Llewellyn's

# 2023 Witches' Companion

A Guide to Contemporary Living

Art Director: Lynne Menturweck
Cover art © Tim Foley
Cover designer: Lynne Menturweck

Interior illustrations:
Tim Foley: 9, 12, 45, 69, 83, 117, 123, 158, 189, 191, 228
Bri Hermanson: 18, 53, 91, 126, 166, 177, 205, 214, 238, 247
M. Kathryn Thompson: 25, 34, 62, 71, 100, 108, 134, 142, 220

ISBN 978-0-7387-6403-0



Llewellyn Publications
A Division of Llewellyn Worldwide Ltd.
2143 Wooddale Drive
Woodbury, MN 55125-2989
www.llewellyn.com

Printed in the United States of America

# Contents

## Community Forum

### Provocative Opinions on Contemporary Topics

## Magical Self-Care

**Nurture Your Body, Mind & Spirit**

## Witchy Living

### Day-by-Day Witchcraft

## Witchcraft Essentials

### Practices, Rituals & Spells

## The Lunar Calendar

**September 2022 to December 2023**

# Community Forum

Provocative Opinions on Contemporary Topics

# Flying Under the Radar: How to Disguise Your Interest in the Craft

*James Kambos*

I have a crystal ball. Genuine crystal. I love to pick it up and feel its heft. Its smoothness. When I'm not scrying with it, I'll stop and admire it. I even love the inclusions trapped inside the otherwise smooth, clear sphere. On the hottest day, it still feels cool to the touch.

But, as I handle it and admire it on this summer afternoon with sunlight streaming through the window, I realize something. If I had possessed a magical tool such as this centuries ago, or any item that could be used for magic, I could have been burned at the stake. Or drowned. Or put on trial for witchcraft. Or ostracized by my community. At the very least, I could have been blamed for a bad harvest—or blamed because Miss Annie's cow down the road stopped giving milk. And who knows what else!

It sounds crazy, doesn't it? But the sad thing is that even now in the twenty-first century, many of us magical folk still have to be careful. How many of you feel the need to hide your magical tools, or anything that could be remotely associated with magic, before family and friends come to visit? Sad but true. Many of us still have to stash away our pointed black hats so we can fly under the radar, as I'm fond of saying, without being detected as a magical practitioner. Even sadder, people other than Witches and Pagans have been targeted. I have even had teachers tell me that they've faced backlash from parents for reading a Harry Potter book aloud in class, or for even having a Harry Potter book in their classroom.

So, just as Witches of times past have had to do, we have to become skillful at blending our magical tools/supplies into our surroundings so we don't raise suspicion that we might be practicing some type of black magic.

**We have to become skillful at blending our magical tools/supplies into our surroundings so we don't raise suspicion that we might be practicing some type of black magic.**

What follows are ideas, tips, and advice on how to live a magical life at home or work, complete with your magical tools at hand—but maybe camouflaged a little. You can still practice your magic and spirituality while flying discreetly under the radar.

To make it easy, I've grouped magical tools and supplies. Under each heading, I give advice on how to use or display your magical items without causing a raised eyebrow. When practical, I also mention how to use some of these items at work.

## Brooms

Brooms, or besoms, as they were once known, are a cleaning tool. But they're also a common magical tool. A broom is also the form of transportation that has traditionally been associated with Witches in occult lore. Being a typical household item, it's a magical tool that can easily be left out in plain view without raising suspicion. Some Witches use their magic broom as a regular cleaning broom as well. They feel it strengthens their connection with their broom. So no one will ever know the broom leaning by your back door is actually a magical broom.

## Candles

Candles are easy to blend into your décor without drawing attention to them as a magical aid. However, you probably won't be able to use them in the workplace, considering the many fire safety codes that are in place. At home, though, candles can easily be both practical and magical. Before burning, simply dress or rub your candles to magically charge them, then safely light before company arrives. Your guests will never know that your candles are working their magic in the background as they burn. Scented candles, even when unlit, can infuse a space with magical energy.

## Cauldrons and Bowls

You may think a cauldron would be hard to disguise as a regular household item, but it isn't. I have an antique, black iron cauldron. I painted the exterior black. When the cauldron is not in magical use, I simply place a potted plant inside of it. Presto—instant planter! When the cauldron is needed on the altar, just remove the potted plant. In the fall, it looks awesome with a potted chrysanthemum sitting in it. The best part is that no one knows its true magical purpose.

Bowls, especially dark bowls, make a great stand-in for a cauldron. And, when filled with water, they double as an effective scrying tool. When an ordinary bowl is left out on the kitchen counter, no one will ever suspect it leads a double life as a magical helper.

## Crystals and Gems

Crystals and semiprecious gems in the form of beads or crystal clusters are highly potent magical tools. Luckily, they're also easy to incorporate into everyday décor. They're very portable as well. If you feel the need for a specific crystal or gem, just put it in your purse or pocket, and you have mobile magical energy. Besides, this is the one magical accessory you can have safely on display at home *or* work. A crystal cluster on your desk or shelf at work won't draw attention to you. Today, many people collect rocks and crystals. Also, the mystical powers of crystals and gems are known and accepted by many non-magical people. You can leave them out at home or work, and no one will know that you've magically charged them. For example, a rose quartz crystal will release calming energy at home or on your desk at work. A dish of aquamarine beads will bring peace to the most stressful home or work environment.

If you're afraid a genuine crystal ball may "out" you as a magical person, try this. In place of a crystal ball, magically charge an attractive glass paperweight. Use it in place of a crystal ball. Glass paperweights are great to use for scrying at home or work.

## Herbs and Flowers

You may have herbs, flowers, or other plants already as houseplants or in the garden. While they aren't exactly a household or magical item, they do have a direct link to magic. For that reason, I think they should be mentioned.

Since most plants have some magical properties, many herbalists and Witches of times past grew cottage gardens overflowing with magical plants. And they did so without fear. Who could tell if those roses spilling over a fence were being raised for their beauty or were leading another life as components in love spells? What about that patch of sage by the kitchen door? Was it only used as a flavoring in tasty recipes? Or, on a moonlit night, was it used to contact spirits of the dead? The point is, herbs and flowers are the one area where you can cut loose and plant them for beauty as well as magic without having to explain. You can also feel safe having potted plants on display at work without drawing attention.

**Herbs and flowers are the one area where you can cut loose and plant them for beauty as well as magic without having to explain. You can also feel safe having potted plants on display at work without drawing attention.**

Drying herbs in your home is another way to activate magical energies without anyone knowing. For instance, drying basil is a good way to banish evil. Mint drying near a window helps to draw protective energies into the home. Hanging a bunch of beautiful yarrow to dry in the home creates a loving atmosphere. It can also be used in love spells.

Dried herbs can also be used to bring calm, protective energy to the workplace without anyone noticing. Here's a situation I found myself in, and how I used dried herbs to change the situation for the better. Years ago, a difficult coworker was fired. After the firing, the entire workplace was filled with tension. That night at home, I blended a mixture of dried sage (a cleanser) and dried rose petals (for calming). I arrived at work early the next morning. I put the herbal mixture in a small dish, placed it in a secluded spot, and said some Words of Power. When anyone asked what it was, I said it was potpourri. The situation improved. We filled the position with a great employee, and I was able to use my magic and my magical supplies while remaining under the radar.

## Final Tips and Tricks

As you've been reading, you've probably thought of some other tricks to disguise your magical ways. Here are a few final tips of my own.

One of the easiest tools to hide in plain sight is a magic mirror. You can use it as an everyday mirror. Then, when it's needed for magic, spray a soft cotton cloth with some bottled spring water and simply wipe the mirror off. This will remove any negative energy from your mirror. Now you can use it as a magic mirror. Also, a small hand mirror kept at work is a great way to deflect any bad vibes coming your way. Just place it so the mirror is facing away from you.

Finally, a word about cards for divining. Tarot cards are a sure sign that you probably practice magic. To avoid this, have you ever thought about learning to read ordinary playing cards? That way you can leave them out, play with them, and divine with them.

..............

It's not easy living a magical life. Until magical folks are completely accepted, we'll have to keep our magic under our pointed hats and fly our magic brooms under the radar.

**James Kambos** *has written essays and articles about folk magic, herbs, and spellcrafting for twenty-five years. He has a degree in the social sciences and geography from Ohio University. He gardens, writes, and paints from his home in the beautiful hill country of southern Ohio.*

**Illustrator: Tim Foley**

# The Ethical Witch and the Noble Quest for Knowledge

*Laura Tempest Zakroff*

At the heart of magic is relationships: how we are connected to the universe and each other and the transfer of energy between us all. Knowledge is an energy exchange. It is offered and received, taught and learned—crafting community and building experience. We can see this exchange clearly in classes and workshops, between teachers and students. But what exchange happens with books and other media?

Books play a major role in learning Witchcraft and magic. I like to refer to Witches and other magical practitioners

as "people of the books." There is no one singular source for inspiration and guidance. There are of course traditions that have a specific book that's been crafted to hold their traditions, rituals, spells, myths, and other practices, but you'd be hard-pressed to find a Witch who believes that should be their sole source of information. Instead, we tend to be bibliophiles with overflowing shelves and nightstands.

Why is that? Because there's always something to learn and books tend to be one of the major accessible sources of information. This particularly became true with the rise of early Modern Witchcraft, where it wasn't so easy to join a coven, discuss the occult out in the open, or find reliable resources.

While reading can't take the place of actual hands-on experience, books can help us get enough of a background and understanding so that we're as prepared as possible and can make smart choices. A good magical herbal can tell you which herbs are safe to use, which are harmful, and what metaphysical attributes they may have.

In addition to books, the internet has brought us a new age of sharing information—for better or worse. It provides a platform for more voices, especially those that have historically been neglected or underrepresented by traditional publishing houses, such as women, people of color, indigenous folks, queer people, etc. The internet has helped to make material more accessible on multiple levels to more people.

**[The internet] provides a platform for more voices, especially those that have historically been neglected or underrepresented by traditional publishing houses, such as women, people of color, indigenous folks, queer people, etc.**

But there's no filter or easy way to determine whether the information you're getting is actually reliable, and now there are new kinds of piracy to watch out for. By piracy, I mean the illegal sharing—and especially the selling—of copyrighted content. What seems like too good a deal usually is, not only leaving the creator high and dry, but often delivering a substandard product to the end user. The energy exchange becomes broken, making it more difficult for folks to put their material out there *and* harder for readers to determine what's real. Being behind a screen makes it easier to forget that real people are being affected.

## Materials to Avoid

To help you make sure the material you're getting is worth your time and money—while also supporting the people who created it in the first place—here is a list of red flags to avoid.

### Pirated PDFs

These show up regularly on sites like Etsy and eBay. Unless an e-book is being offered on those sites for direct sale by the author themselves (*and* the work is typically self-published as well), it's very likely an illegal copy. Neither the author nor the publishing house is compensated when e-books are sold this way.

### Foul Fakes

Forged copies of books and especially Tarot decks have been making the rounds lately. These are cheaply made knockoffs of the actual work, sold for a fraction of the price. If that bargain deck is missing a booklet or some cards, the binding is falling apart on the book, or the pages seem extra thin or misprinted, you've been duped. Not only does this hurt the creators, but you're getting an inferior product as well.

### Phantom Books

These tend to be books that are more flash than substance, typically available only online. They often use fake names that sound similar to established authors in the genre, and the content is often plagiarized—swiped from websites or other books without much care for accuracy. These books target newbies and try to cash in on trends. Possible clues include scant information about the author or publishing house, multiple books released all at once recently, very low page counts, etc. If you're unsure about a book, check to see if you can find that title anywhere else or know anyone who's read it.

## Quality Resources

Now that we've got that out of the way, here is a list of resources that won't break your budget while providing quality material to study.

### Free Public Library

If you haven't been to your local library in a while, get thee to their website! Even if your local branch doesn't have the book you're looking for on its shelves, it's part of a larger system that may. You can request books to be delivered to your local branch and held for you. Most libraries also have e-book services. I like to check a book out of the library first to see if it's what I need and then purchase a copy if I want to add it to my library. Libraries pay for the books they loan, so the author and publisher are getting compensated.

### Private Libraries

These are specialized libraries that may require a donation or membership fee. There's quite a few occult libraries out there that are easily found with a quick google search. You can also check with established traditions who may also have a lending library as part of their resources.

### Used and Bargain Bookshops

Most of my early books came from used book stores, partly because I loved discovering whatever was there and partly because I was broke AF. They're also often independent small businesses that are a vibrant part of the local community. Bargain bookshops often sell new books that have been slightly damaged in some way (or discontinued), so the publisher wholesales them at a bulk discount. Sometimes you can get quite a deal! You can also check out these used book websites: AbeBooks.com, BetterWorldBooks.com, alibris.com, Powells.com, or Thriftbooks.com.

### Copyright-Free Websites

Many older occult books are now in the public domain, so you can read them online for free. Try the Internet Sacred Text Archive (www.sacred-texts.com) and the Hermetic Library (www.hermetic.com).

### Affordable Subscriptions

There are several online services that you can try for free and then subscribe at a low monthly rate that enables you to have access to a huge amount of material. Two options are Scribd, scribd.com, and Kindle Unlimited, https://www.amazon.com/kindle-dbs/hz/subscribe/ku.

## What about New Physical Books, Though?

My preferred way to find new material is from my local independent bookstore or favorite Witch/metaphysical shop. Sure I could maybe save a couple of dollars online, but having a local shop to visit that directly supports my community is worth far more in the long run. They're the places that hold events, teach classes, carry local artisans' work, and employ folks in your community. These shops can usually order anything you want as well.

Another great option is buying directly from the author (if available), and that can also score you a signed copy! Check their social media to see if they have an online shop.

If there's nothing local to you, try bookshop.org, a website that helps independent bookshops sell their wares online. You can even support your favorite little shop a state away if they're on there!

There are other ways you can help support authors, artists, and other creators. One of the best things to do is to post a review (such as on Amazon, Goodreads, etc.) or share a photo/video on your social media telling others what you liked or found helpful about the book, deck, podcast, or project. Creators can try to promote their work nonstop, but research has shown that folks often go with what their peers, friends, and family recommend. A simple review might not seem like much, but it works!

Lastly, an important thing to know is that the money you invest in books and other media craft the market. What you see on the shelves is largely the result of demand. Share with your favorite bookseller the authors and topics you want to see, and make a conscious effort to support creators who are underrepresented. You are a part of the energy exchange, which means you play an active role in crafting the wisdom of your community. Happy reading!

**Laura Tempest Zakroff** *is a professional artist, author, performer, and Modern Traditional Witch based in New England. She holds a BFA from RISD (the Rhode Island School of Design), and her artwork has received awards and honors worldwide. Her work embodies myth and the esoteric through her drawings and paintings, jewelry, talismans, and other designs. Laura is the author of the bestselling Llewellyn books* Weave the Liminal, Sigil Witchery, *and* Anatomy of a Witch, *as well as the* Liminal Spirits Oracle *and* Anatomy of a Witch Oracle *(artist/author). She is the creative force behind several community events and teaches workshops online and worldwide. Visit her at www.LauraTempestZakroff.com.*

**Illustrator: Bri Hermanson**

# Extremist Groups in Paganism

*Charlynn Walls*

Extremist groups are found in every facet of life, including religious movements and political arenas. Some extremist individuals and groups can appear to be less obtrusive than others, but it is a sad reality that we will all be touched by one at some point in our lives, even if only tangentially. As Pagans, we must use our knowledge and expertise to identify and uproot the extremists that we find in our midst, because unfortunately we as a group are often judged based on those in our community who have the loudest voice, not those who are in the majority.

We have seen instances in the media of individuals in the Pagan community who have their own hidden agenda. Recently we had a group identifying itself as following a Norse path that was aligned with the white supremacy movement. We also saw a self-identified Pagan individual participate in the insurrection at the US Capitol Building in Washington, DC, on January 6, 2021.

While Pagans have strived for religious acceptance and inclusion, fighting against these images can be difficult. It often sets back the progress that has been made and then we must regroup and try to regain lost ground.

## What Does an Extremist Group Look Like?

Extremist groups and individuals often share several characteristics that will help you identify them. An extremist will feel that their way is the only one. They will be divisive and try to silence those with whom they disagree. Individuals or groups with extremist viewpoints will also be prepared to fight a final battle for these beliefs. Let's break down these points in more detail so you are prepared to see these people for who they truly are.

Recruitment is at the front of their minds, and extremists will seek out individuals who are already marginalized and looking to belong. This can make those seeking a connection to spirit through Paganism especially vulnerable, since they are already looking for a community where they can thrive. The extremist will attend events not to participate, but to seek out others they feel can be indoctrinated into their beliefs/cause. At first they may seem like perfectly normal, reasonable people. So how do you recognize when you are interacting with an extremist?

Groups or individuals who have extreme viewpoints often hide in plain sight. They may seem overly eccentric when you first meet them. Most of us will have a feeling that something is "off" about them, even if we aren't quite sure what it is. You should honor those gut feelings, as they are usually accurate. You will notice that the person talks in absolutes, and there are no gray areas with them. Also, they feel that they are always in the right. If you should happen to disagree with them, you become a target for their verbal aggression.

These individuals or groups will be exclusionary. I know what you're already saying to yourself: "But most Pagan groups are selective." Well, *selective* and *exclusionary* are not the same thing. *Selective* means you're looking for the best fit for your group based on people's personalities and practices. Pagan groups also tend to be small, which means that openings aren't always available when we'd like them to be. However, *exclusionary* means you refuse to include others based on a qualifier beyond their control, such as race or ethnicity.

**Predatory groups and individuals will also attempt to isolate you from others. They want to be the only influence in your life. Rather than trying to build community and camaraderie, they constantly tear down others around them.**

Predatory groups and individuals will also attempt to isolate you from others. They want to be the only influence in your life. Rather than trying to build community and camaraderie, they constantly tear down others around them. These individuals and groups will not want you to continue to broaden your perspective or be inclusive of others. For example, they would actively discourage you from traveling to a Pagan festival to participate in lectures and group activities in order to broaden your horizons.

Extremists will, over time, reveal their true agenda to you and/or the community at large. They may be a radical individual or group that believes it is okay to use force to gain what they feel is their right or will further their cause. Escalating violence against others while filtering it through the lens of their religious beliefs is a scary prospect, one that is fraught with problems.

## How Extremist Groups Impact the Community

Community impact is a huge factor when faced with an extremist group. The impact often is twofold for those within the Pagan community. The first issue is, of course, the fracturing of community. The community is being attacked from within, and that is difficult to combat. In a healthy community, we may not all have the same belief structure, but we honor the fact that you have found a soul-enriching path that is outside of mainstream, accepted pathways. When we have extremists in our midst, they will attempt to pit us against one another, so that they are the only remaining choice in the area. That makes recruitment easier for them, and they never have to lift a finger.

The second issue is the impact on the larger community around us. Many of us have had to live in areas where we are in the broom closet due to the issues our communities have with Paganism. When an extremist group identifies as a Pagan group, that is the face that becomes associated with Paganism. The louder the voice, the more recognition they get. It's certainly not fair, but that is what tends to happen. Then it becomes guilt by association as they become the face or the voice of our religious path. Damage control in these situations is best accomplished through service and outreach projects, but getting such efforts established or reestablished can take time and persistence.

## What to Do if You Come Across an Extremist Group in Your Community

You might have to walk a fine line when you have an extremist group in your community. So what can you do to combat their presence and influence?

First, build community. If you have a thriving Pagan community where individuals and groups work well together, there is less room for a divisive group to move in. Discord and chaos are what these groups thrive on. They seek to destroy those that are open and respectful of other groups and pathways. If we come together, we remove one of the most useful tools in their arsenal.

As an individual, you can have conversations with others that bring to light what is happening. Don't be afraid to speak up and shine a light on them with others in your community. This, of course, shouldn't devolve into a "he said, she said" situation. Stick to the facts and let others make up their own minds.

If you are someplace where there are many people present (like at a study group) or are in a public area (like a coffee shop) for a meeting, and someone brings up something that you recognize as coming from an extremist viewpoint and it is making you uncomfortable, try not to respond with nervous laughter. That will be interpreted as compliance or as acceptance of what they are saying.

I know we've all been in a situation like that. The best way to try to defuse the situation is to ask them, "What are you doing?" This will make them rethink what they are saying, along with how it is being perceived. They may not answer you immediately, because they will be stunned that you responded to them with a question, so you can then repeat the phrase. Doing so will often shut down the negative behavior. However, please *never* confront the group or individual by yourself if you can avoid it, as it can exacerbate the problem and provide them an excuse to escalate the situation and resort to violence.

If you are part of a group, then one recommendation is to reach out to other groups in the area that you are aware of and see if they have had similar issues. You will often find that they have indeed had similar concerns. While it may not always be feasible due to how spread out your community is, calling a conclave of group representatives to meet, discuss the situation, and determine a course of action for your community would be one solution. If they can provide some guidance to the community on the situation as a united force, that is powerful. If they can agree to ban any events that the extremist groups run in your area, then it limits the number of people they have access to and could potentially recruit to their cause.

If the extremist group is becoming more virulent and you expect that their behavior may escalate to violence of some type toward others within the community, you can and should notify the authorities. Again, they will expect you to have some facts to support your concern and will ask you why you feel the group has become a threat. Be prepared to answer some hard questions if you go this route. A lot of people will feel it isn't their place to do so. However, if we truly walk our talk and it is a matter of saving lives, you owe it to yourself and your community to proceed.

## Magical Recourse

As practitioners of magical paths, what can we do about extremism in a magical capacity? While we can do protective and reflective magic to help counteract these types of groups, it should be utilized in conjunction with the previously described practical strategies. One type of magical defense is to use mirrors to reflect their negativity back onto themselves. Take a small mirror and place it near the front door of your home or your group meeting place. Set the mirror with the intention of allowing any and all negativity to be reflected back to those sending that energy your way.

You can also put an extremist in a magical timeout by putting their name, their group name, or an item associated with them in the freezer. I prefer to use a small ziplock bag for this purpose. I write down the name along with what action I want to stop. I also like to include a time frame for the work, because I cannot leave this in my freezer indefinitely. For instance, if I wanted a group to stop trying to create a rift between my group and the rest of the community, I would write that they will not be able to do so for a period of three months. I would also include that over the next month the spell will gradually fade, so that a reevaluation of the situation can be explored. This allows me to take the bag out of the freezer after the "freeze" period and dispose of it, because I have already considered the period of time needed for the tapering off of the spell. I know that some people would want to bind the individual or group so that they are no longer a threat, but I would steer clear of doing binding magic on a group of this type. Bindings tend to be a more permanent solution, and I simply would not want to tie them energetically to myself.

. . . . . . . . . . . . .

While the hope is that we never have to deal with a group or an individual who is part of an extremist group that is claiming to be Pagan, it is a possibility. You need to know what to do should the situation arise. Extremism and violence have no part in our world, and we have a duty to make sure we all feel safe in our communities.

**Charlynn Walls** *is an active member of her local community and a member of a local area coven. A practitioner of the Craft for over twenty years, she currently resides in central Missouri with her family. Charlynn continues to expand on her Craft knowledge and practices daily. She enjoys sharing her knowledge by teaching online and at local festivals and by writing articles for publication with Llewellyn.*

**Illustrator: M. Kathryn Thompson**

# The Controversial Pagan: Issues of Ethics, Power, and Insensitivity

*Susan Pesznecker*

Those of us who've been active in the Pagan community for any period of time have inevitably run into people or issues that raised questions of ethics, kindness, human behavior, or even morality. Consider, for example, the inappropriate use of culturally sensitive practices and materials, the elder who wields power and is more narcissist than teacher, and the novice who is treated more like a slave than a student.

In this regard, Pagans are no different from everyone else, and these issues certainly aren't unique to us. We're human. We have human foibles. We can be rude, greedy, unkind, and lustful. Of course we can also be generous, kind, discreet, and polite. But like all humans, we often need reminders of how to conduct ourselves, especially when confronted with actions that violate a reasonable and civilized norm.

**[Pagans] can also be generous, kind, discreet, and polite. But like all humans, we often need reminders of how to conduct ourselves, especially when confronted with actions that violate a reasonable and civilized norm.**

Let me start by defining what I mean by the term *Pagan*. I'm using this as an umbrella term to describe those of us who follow nontraditional belief systems, many of which are rooted in nature and the natural world. The key in my definition, though, is that we're typically not part of the "big tent" religions, and in fact we're often somewhat suspicious of them, whether because of their proselytizing, their exclusivity, their narrow view of human rights, their often-patriarchal structure, and more. That said, I know many Pagans who also follow a mainstream religion, including a Cherokee shaman who is a lifelong member of the Church of England and a Gardnerian Wiccan baptized in the Episcopal Church and still following some of those tenets. This raises another canon of Paganism: tolerance. I feel like since we've all gone out of the way to forge our own paths, most of us are extra tolerant of spiritual diversity in all its forms. Usually.

Note, too, that I'm capitalizing the word Pagan because I feel it represents specific spiritual practices, even if they differ. But I'm not capitalizing words like grove or coven or circle because there is so much diversity there that it's safer and more equitable to use the common noun expression.

In writing this article, I was asked not to rely on source materials and scholarship but to share my own experiences and insights over several decades of practice, and that's what I did. If you find yourself disagreeing with some of my ideas here, I hope you'll know they're being presented honestly. You might consider why you're disagreeing. I'm not saying I'm right and you're wrong; I'm just saying that sometimes we behave way too much like, well…humans: quick to make assumptions and not always very good about checking the actual facts.

Let's dive in.

## Secrecy and Fair Treatment

Many Pagan belief systems and practices are shrouded in secrecy, with information being revealed or released to initiates as they progress in their knowledge and skill or as they move through degrees, levels, circles, or periods of time. I don't think there's anything wrong with this, provided the same tests and expectations are given to all and the same material is provided to everyone. After all, some groups' materials and practices are bound by oath or tradition.

But when secrecy becomes a tool of power used to cajole or control, we've gone off the rails. I had a personal experience with an elder who was working with a young member toward an initiation. There was some friction when the excited newbie was moving a little more quickly than the elder thought she should (note that there was no rule prescribing speed-of-movement), and thus as she completed each step, the elder required even more of her, moving the goalposts and demanding more time, more work, etc.

The youngster was doing high-quality work and was bubbling with enthusiasm, but the elder, having simply decided it was too much, too fast, finally all but locked the initiate down. It was unfair and unreasonable, and it resulted in the Druid grove losing a potentially wonderful new member. This particular elder sat on the grove's governing group and steamrolled over others' questions and requests for explanation until the group gave up, sighed deeply, and allowed the vibrant new member to slip away rather than deal directly with the rather obnoxious elder.

What would you have done if you'd been in that governing group?

## Power-Hungry Leadership

We all know the type: the world is filled with people who enjoy being in positions of power. We see this daily on the news. In the previous example, a Druid elder abused her position of power simply because of a personal issue—and because she *could*. There was nothing and no one constraining her, including her own sense of right and wrong. What *was* motivating her was a thirst for power over someone else.

People handle power differently. Some hold powerful positions out of a desire to do good works. They wear the mantle well, give generously, and are held in high regard. They're the ones who know how to lead—as in, when a hole needs to be dug, they're at the front of the line setting the example, calling, "Give me a shovel."

But alas, too often empowered people live for the ego trip. Rather than teaching, collaborating, or working toward shared accomplishments, they veer toward bossiness, manipulation, or overwork or even abuse of subordinates, and then they take all the credit for the end result. They enjoy building a long list of titles and accomplishments, but only for the accolades—not so much for the work involved.

I think again of a Druid grove where one senior member demanded the title of Arch Druid. The grove had no bylaws providing for such a role, nor was there any function for it. In the history of the grove, there had never been an Arch Druid. But this elder demanded it, was given the title (mostly because the other leaders simply wanted to pacify her so she'd stop complaining), and then immediately began acting as if she was newly in charge of all operations. Why did the other elders allow this? They ignored her at first, not knowing how to undo what they'd put into action. They also knew her, and knew that when opposed, she would make life unpleasant for everyone. But eventually they tired of her power games and began resisting. She eventually left the grove under some pressure, but of course she claimed her departure was everyone else's fault. Soon after, she created her own grove where she could make the rules and reign unchallenged.

How would you handle a similar abuse of power, assuming you were in a position to have an impact? What can groups do to prevent this sort of exploitation?

## Mistreatment of Newbies and Novices

Any time a newbie enters a coven, they take a leap of faith. Hopefully they've done their homework and determined in advance that the group is a good fit, but as we all know, some of this doesn't become clear until one is inside. For many, the experience is wonderful. But reports too often surface about newbies who are taken advantage of.

For several years I worked in an online school of magic with a woman who led a coven in the Midwest. The coven adhered to a three-circle system, and initiates who entered were outside all three. Again, that's all well and good as long as fairness is at play and the newbie knows what's up. But things quickly became a bit shady with this coven. On days of sabbat, esbat, ritual, or even simple meetings, newbies would be expected to show up early that day to cook, clean house, and...wait for it...do the high priestess's laundry. No joke. Note that *none* of this had anything to do with the rituals or practices being held. I mean, if they had been asked to set up an altar and dress candles and such, that would have made sense. But washing someone's undies?

Also, if these "younglings" resisted, even for a second, what do you think happened? Yup: they were *out*.

"Ah," some might say, "this is the way we've always done it. We suffered a little and now it's their turn. We made it through and they'll make it through. It builds character. After all, we want to make sure they *really* want in."

Welcome to the Land of Hazing! The Oxford Dictionary defines hazing as "the imposition of strenuous, often humiliating, tasks as part of a program of rigorous physical training and initiation." I'd say being forced to mop someone's kitchen floor and wash their underwear qualifies as hazing, wouldn't you? And think about it: if you wanted this person to become an engaged, productive member of your group, would you start by demeaning them? I think not.

As a teacher both in and out of the magical realm, I have a special spot for students. Students thirst for knowledge. They come to us like open books—sometimes skeptical books, but books all the same. And they come seeking knowledge. Taking advantage of students not only is morally wrong but also crosses the line between teacher and student and veers from the path of knowledge into the path of brutishness.

**Taking advantage of students not only is morally wrong but also crosses the line between teacher and student and veers from the path of knowledge into the path of brutishness. Indeed, effective teaching is all about respect.**

Indeed, effective teaching is all about respect. A good teacher gives generously to their students. We have no expectation other than opening the student's mind a bit and thirsting them to ask, "What's next?" And, of tremendous importance, teachers also learn from their students. Respect grows in both directions as part of the process. But this requires a level playing field and the building of enough trust to sustain vulnerability.

What would you do if you knew the leader of your group was forcing new members to wash their floors, mow their lawn, and do their laundry? Especially when it had nothing to do with the group's work? How would you respond to the "it's always been like this" argument? Do you consider that a viable argument?

## Fundamentalism and Elitism: My Way Is the Right Way

Ah, that day when you bump into a fundamentalist, the "my way or the highway" type...These folks believe their way is the right way, and they have a hard time entertaining other approaches—or find it completely impossible to do so.

At the start of this essay, I mentioned that most of us Pagan types are extra tolerant of spiritual diversity. But note I said "most." Sadly, fundamentalists hide among us. Fundamentalism is absolutely a kind of gatekeeping. You must believe in these gods to join. You must be willing to follow these absolute rules and routines or you can't join. You must carry out this ritual with absolutely no variation if you wish to remain a member. What if, after a person's own immersion, study, and personal gnosis, they veer off in a slightly different direction and, horrors, start asking questions or, gasp, challenging the group norms?

Is this type of fundamentalist approach always wrong? There are certain traditions in which prescribed rituals and practices are literally followed to the letter. This is their way, and a person joining one of these groups must be prepared for what they're stepping into. Alas, fundamentalism can quickly become a kind of elitism, where members of a group hold a particular set of attitudes and anyone who doesn't share those attitudes and isn't willing to toe the line is treated poorly. In the best cases, groups welcome these challenges as a chance to examine, explore, and perhaps strengthen their own ideas and positions. In the worst cases, it results in bad feelings and severed relationships and can erode the group's reputation in their local magic community.

This sort of elitism also tends to drive away new members, which is never good, as a group only grows and endures with the energy and ideas of new members. Fundamentalists can be nitpicky, too. People who make fun of others for mispronouncing Samhain or argue about whether Imbolc should be celebrated on January 31 or February 1 won't win any popularity contests, and these types of behavior may result in groups losing potential members who had a lot to offer.

How would you deal with a new member who questioned your group's beliefs and practices? What would you do if you saw another member shutting down the questions?

## Big Name Pagans and Fallen Idols

Let's consider our Pagan elders, the ones who have been around for years—even decades—with noteworthy involvement in the Craft, whether as leaders, teachers, writers, artists, or the like. They're known for giving tremendous service to all things Pagan. They've earned the renown and even the comfortable adulation of those they've worked with. They give generously, ask for little in return, and are often loved openly by a great many people.

But sometimes they go too far. Enter the Big Name Pagan, or BNP. Some people use BNP as a general acronym, but more often I hear it said with sarcasm and absolutely *not* as a compliment. In such cases, the BNP is the tertiary step for a power-hungry leader. Their name and visage have not simply gained wider acclaim but have lofted them to the level of guru. You've seen it: they attend a gathering and everyone wants to stand close to them or talk to them or take a selfie or in some way worship in their presence.

So what's the problem with this? Is there anything wrong with fawning over a Pagan celebrity? After all, with social media and influencer culture, that's how the world works these days, right?

**Is there anything wrong with fawning over a Pagan celebrity?... Too often the BNP guru spirals into guru worship, and this all too easily leads to exploitation of "underlings."**

Unfortunately, too often the BNP guru spirals into guru worship, and this all too easily leads to exploitation of "underlings," who are inevitably vulnerable and, feeling powerless in the shadow of the guru, may feel compelled to do whatever the guru asks. Cultism, anyone? Let's look at some specific examples:

- The BNP who asks their disciples to provide money, a place to live, etc.—Asking for help in a crisis is very human and certainly isn't wrong! But when one expects support, cash, etc., that's something different—and no different from a cult leader who expects to be idolized.
- The BNP who makes a claim about their experiences that is untrue or exaggerated simply to bolster their image
- The BNP who diverts funds that were given to a group for a specific purpose and then uses them for personal gain

Bottom line: We're all people. We're all walking life's path together, and celebrity worship, false gods, and fetishism aren't appropriate—even though social media sometimes seems to push us in that direction these days.

What would you do if confronted by a BNP who was clearly abusing their power? What if you saw a friend or fellow practitioner falling under the sway of one of these people?

Sadly, there's an even darker side to this, such as the BNP who becomes a fallen idol. Stories regularly surface of BNPs who are implicated in sexual assault, theft, or other crimes. I recall discovering that the author of a much-loved Arthurian text had been involved in a decades-long practice of child sexual abuse. What would you do if you found out the person who wrote your favorite text or piece of music or is a leader in your magical tradition committed a dark, heinous act? Could you separate the person from the material? Is that possible?

## Cultural Appropriation

I couldn't conclude this essay without discussing cultural appropriation. Simply put, cultural appropriation is when a member of one culture adopts and uses the customs, practices, religious rituals, or other elements of another culture or identity. To better understand this concept, let's consider a few examples:

- A white person making a ritual robe out of African kente cloth
- Culturally insensitive Halloween costumes—for example, dressing as a member of another race or culture when one doesn't belong to that race or culture
- Using or wearing cultural artifacts or garb when not part of that culture—for example, wearing a Native American headdress or an Indian bindi
- Adopting blackface (*never* okay)
- Referring to having a "spirit animal" or "totem" or calling oneself a shaman—labels and roles with specific religious connotations within indigenous cultures

- Carrying out a practice that belongs to indigenous people, such as smudging

Why are these practices a problem? At the very least, they're disrespectful. It's taking a practice that's part of another's traditions and heritage and using it out of context. It's a kind of cultural looting, really. To make it even worse, the cultural "appropriator" often belongs to a dominant culture, meaning they're co-opting material that belongs to a minority or marginalized group.

The problem also applies to using culturally sensitive materials, including white sage. Different cultures and indigenous peoples use these materials as part of their traditional practices. An outsider's use of these items not only is inappropriate but in some cases is part of overuse that has led to scarcity of the material. It's better to find substitutes, such as using garden sage, wormwood, or rosemary instead of white sage. Also, we must be sensitive in our choice of terms referring to culturally traditional practices; for example, using the terms *cleansing* or *clearing* instead of *smudging* or *saging*.

• • • • • • • • • • • • • •

None of us is perfect, and we all stumble occasionally. But if we aim to treat one another with honesty, kindness, and respect, and if we're generous of spirit, we'll get there.

**Susan Pesznecker** *is a mother, grandmother, writer, nurse, and college English professor living in the beautiful green Pacific Northwest with her poodles. An initiated Druid, green magick devoteé, and amateur herbalist, Sue loves reading, writing, cooking, travel, and anything having to do with the outdoors. Her previous works include* Crafting Magick with Pen and Ink, The Magickal Retreat, *and* Yule: Recipes & Lore for the Winter Solstice. *Follow her on Instagram as Susan Pesznecker.*

**Illustrator: M. Kathryn Thompson**

# Black Magick and Why We Need It

*Stephanie Rose Bird*

When I came of age in the late 1970s, there were few books available to the typical reader about Black Magick, and by that I mean magick practiced by African-descended people. This lack of accessibility to my people's magick brought a heaviness to my heart. I wanted to practice. I had the calling. It was essential to include the ways of my ancestors in my spiritual practice, and not just the magick that was readily available. I've learned that this desire for knowledge and the opportunity to immerse oneself in Black Magick strikes

many people. This essay is about how I found Black Magick and why we all need it.

As a bookish sort of person, an absence of information on African-American and African-inspired magick put me in a quandary when I was growing up. I did two things when my go-tos, the library and bookstores, did not yield the information that I felt was essential to my development. I delved into European-based witchcraft through my friends who were witches. After all, some of my ancestry is based in Europe, though the majority is African. My second strategy was to open my eyes wide and see what I could ferret out and ultimately discover around me. I believed firmly that the ancestors and spirits wanted me, a young Black woman, to stay on the path of magick. I figured they could see the awkward situation I found myself in and would help me.

I have always been open to the spiritual practices around me, be they Native American, European, African, Asian, or other paths. I mention these particular paths because they were the ones around me, for one reason or another. For example, there were hex signs found in neighboring counties on barns and outbuildings, which are favored by the Pennsylvania Dutch but are actually Germanic in origin. Even back in the 1970s, there were compilations of Native American healing ways to be had, with minimal searching. Hatha yoga was important to me as a young teen, and this opened me up to some of the Asian philosophies and metaphysics. Still, my family, mixed with other cultures, was my primary hunting ground for information on Black Magick. They were grounded in organized religions.

## Abrahamic Faiths

Finding diversity in our spirituality is a blessing. I noticed this early on. Yes, we were Protestants: Baptists, Apostolic Christians, and various Methodists. We had a portion of the family who were called "Black" Muslims at the time. My uncle was married to a Yoruba tribal woman from Nigeria, adding more rich texture to our stew. She was practicing the African traditional religions (ATRs) of her people. At the same time, my uncle seemed to walk a very curious idiosyncratic path, at least when compared to the so-called organized or Abrahamic faiths to which I was more accustomed. We had a triracial, predominantly Native American family member who seemed impartial to religion altogether, and an atheist uncle. So to quench my thirst, I investigated the spirituality within the Baptists, Apostolic Christians, and Methodists. As a child, I believed in following the majority.

## Speaking in Tongues and Getting Happy

In Christianity, two curiosities for me were speaking in tongues and getting happy. Speaking in tongues suggests spiritual possession, not unlike the mounting that the spirits do in various African-inspired types of spirituality such as Haitian Vodoun and primarily Brazilian Candomblé. People speak unknown or unfamiliar languages and sometimes words that are not familiar to them when speaking in tongues. It was my great-grandmother, whom we called Vafawn, who would get enraptured in biblical texts and speak in tongues, mainly in the closet, and I do mean that quite literally. VaFawn's behavior was odd, disorienting, and somewhat scary to observe as a youth, but through it I learned about some of the depth and weird offshoots of Christianity, a faith that otherwise seemed on the mundane side to me.

Another activity or event I noticed was the gathering of women dressed entirely in white (again, a throwback to some of the other practices in the African diaspora) around someone in a state of ecstasy that we call *getting happy*. Getting happy harkens across the Atlantic to places in our African lineage where people get overcome by spirits, mostly spirit animals and various types of entities. I speak here of how the spirits mount humans in Vodoun and are cultivated and invited to mount the Candomblé practitioner.

> **There are deeply moving spiritual activities in our Black churches that call to the spirit of many parishioners. The spiritual expression ranges from soul-stirring gospel songs, clapping, and rocking back and forth to the call-and-response of the reverend with the congregation.**

My mother would catch the spirit regularly when we went to church together as a family. She would shuffle back and forth and tremble, sometimes as though having a seizure. She'd raise her arms skyward to receive the Holy Spirit. Her display was both mortifying and attractive. Sometimes I joined in with her. When I got older and was in a gospel choir, I'd get happy too.

While there might not seem like there is obvious or earth-shattering magick going on around you, you may well find it in the most straight-laced of places, like in your church. There are deeply moving spiritual activities in our Black churches that call to the spirit of many parishioners. The spiritual expression ranges from soul-stirring gospel songs, clapping, and rocking back and forth to the call-and-response of the minister or reverend with the congregation. You can be moved and engage in Black Magick pretty close to home and somewhat discreetly.

## Astrology

As a curious child, I was always observant, not only reading what I could find that was metaphysical but also watching what those around me did. My parents, who would never call themselves metaphysical or Pagan, God forbid, were quite into astrology. Astrology swung open another heavyweight door for me. *What was all of this about the signs, the stars, the planets, and sky-going happenings?* I wondered about this in the thick, dark cover of the night at times and under the moon's bright light at others.

My parents had a craft shop, and we sold all manner of zodiac signs to customers, probably from various religions. Astrology opened me up to something more significant than the mundane world, grounded in earthly concerns. There were forces at play, and I wanted to understand how they worked. Moreover, observing the phases of the moon, watching the moon's effect on the tides of the lake and occasionally the sea, and feeling the moon's effects on myself opened yet another door to mystical powers.

## Atmospheric Shifts

An interesting type of Black Magick I observed and benefited from is something I call atmospheric shifts. My mother sparked these atmospheric shifts through what is commonly referred to as aromatherapy. Black folk have practiced various types of aromatherapy since Egyptian times, particularly with attention to African resin incenses such as frankincense, myrrh, and copal, and highly fragrant oils. We believe strongly in shifting the atmosphere of our living spaces through aroma and scenting, using pine products—something near and dear to us since Early American times. We continue to use the resins frankincense and myrrh for their practical ability to uplift and their connection to the Bible, as well as camphor-rich products to relieve chest colds and the deleterious effects of body aches.

Luck is brought into play often, and in its own way is an atmospheric shift. I watched my mother throw pennies when we moved to a new home and have done lengthy research into the practice, connecting it to Hoodoo blessings, spiritual offerings, and invocation of the ancestor's goodwill.

## Alternative Spirituality

As I did my observations growing up, I saw that there were other intense practices in my orbit, with my uncle's Yoruba wife and with his predilection for Santeria. Coming and going to my uncle's summer place, I observed evidence of an altar to Eshu Elegua. I saw the remnants of sacrificed chicken rituals and noticed that my uncle's dress was distinctive, including a white robe-like garb and red beads. It wasn't long until he shared his connection to Shango, whom I've since learned I should tread around very respectfully. The orishas of my uncle's Santeria practice opened up a new magickal way of looking at the world.

One of my cousins was into the Craft, metaphysics, and alchemy. He hipped me to Albertus Magnus, an alchemist from hundreds of years ago. Magnus's writings are well respected in the African-American folkloric practice I gravitated to, called Hoodoo.

## Magick Making

Of course, there is a lot of fear of the unknown, the dark, and the mysterious. Black folks, in some cases, fit into those categories in the minds of those who make no effort to get to know us. Black Magick in particular, then, has been historically outlawed, punishable by death in some states during enslavement and afterward, restricted, and generally forbidden. Still to this day, I have to argue for pairing the words *Black* and *Magick* because of its double entendre. The use of the term Black Magick has a dark and negative connotation, which is insulting.

The thing is, we need Black folk's magick. We need Black Magick, just like we need every other type of magick from the cultures of the rainbow. Sticking to my point, Black Magick empowers a group of people who have been disenfranchised, disempowered, persecuted, and derided. Practices like Hoodoo and Vodoun lend empowerment and self-determination. Through practicing these paths, we can deal with everyday problems, reach out to our ancestors, and be attentive to spirits and entities around us.

Black Magick might seem to be headquartered far away in distant lands in the various sub-Saharan countries of Africa, and we see it elsewhere in the African diaspora. But Black Magick is also right here in the United States. It is in our churches and other places of worship, in our homes, living in our relatives and not just our ancestors. Black Magick is given voice through our keen interest in storytelling, oration, singing, folklore, mythology, and spirits. Just as Black people are beautiful, Black Magick is gorgeous, needed, and a national treasure. Where would we be without some good mojo? Black people know we have vibed and indeed survived off the spirit of magick. We, as a people, need Black Magick, and so do you!

**Stephanie Rose Bird** *has written for the Llewellyn annuals, including* Llewellyn's Spell-A-Day Almanac, *as well as four Llewellyn books, including the award-winning and best-selling* Sticks, Stones, Roots & Bones *and* 365 Days of Hoodoo. *Her soon-to-be published Llewellyn title,* Spirits in My Bones, *focuses on deep ancestry practices. She has several other books published on magick and anthropology and is also the author of several magical realism fantasy YA novels. Bird is an eclectic pagan practicing shamanism, green witchcraft, and hoodoo. Bird, her husband, family, and animals live in Chicagoland. Her website is www.stephanierosebird.com. Follow her on Instagram @s.r.bird, Twitter @stephanierosebi, and Facebook at https://www.facebook.com/stephanierosebirdauthor.*

**Illustrator: Tim Foley**

# Recreating Our Personal Magic Circles: Let's Update Our Magic!

*Barbara Ardinger*

Two years ago in the *2021 Witches' Companion* I wrote that we Pagans don't have to do everything the old, traditional way and suggested that we can look at the Wheel of the Year in a different way. I've heard from readers of the Llewellyn annuals that they liked that idea. Now I ask, what else can we do to make our magic more personal?

Let's come home again and look at the circles in which we do our magical work. We know the Received Wiccan Wisdom about these circles. You cast your circle, generally starting in the north, and move yourself and/or your wand or athame

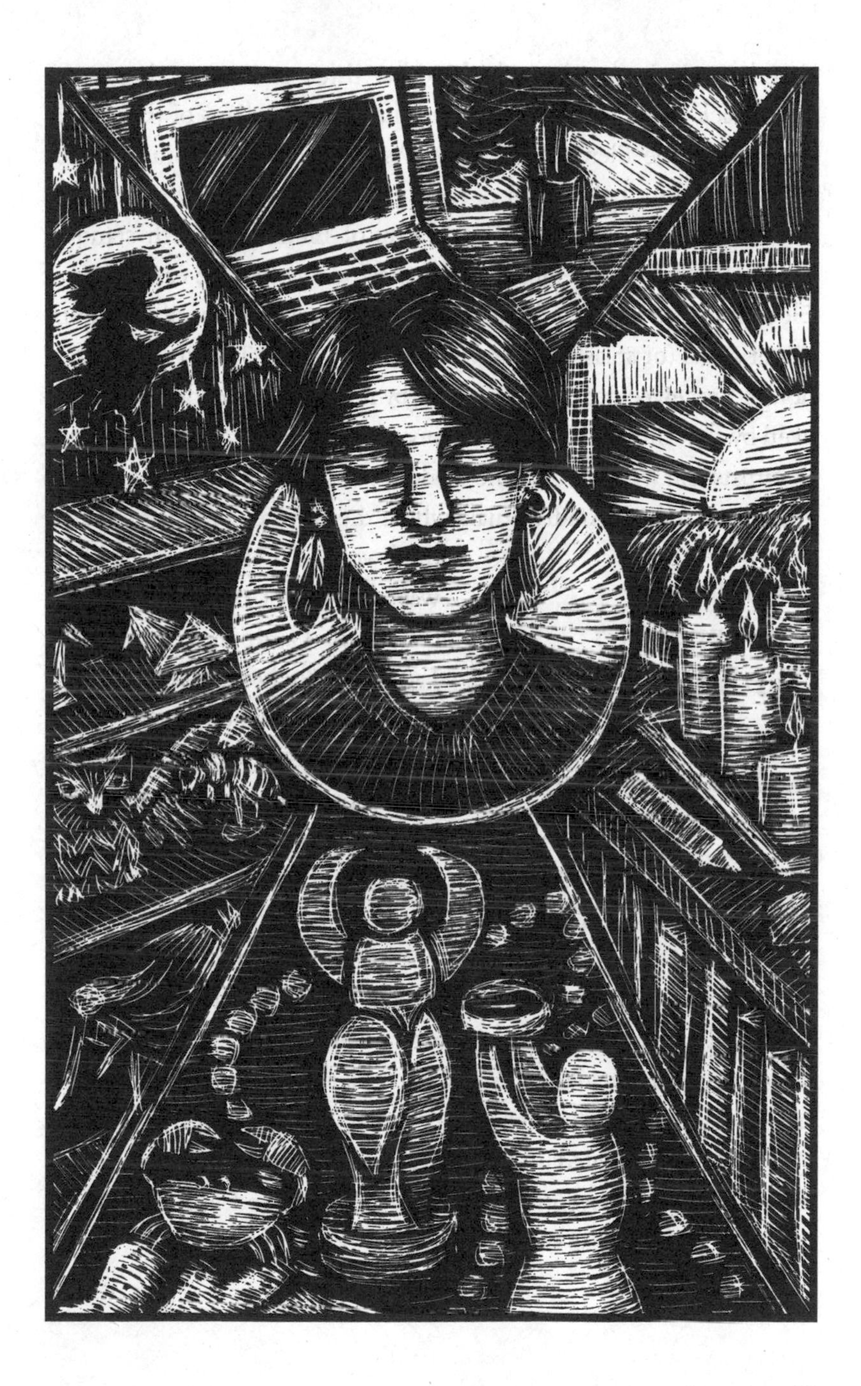

deosil, or clockwise, through the other three directions, closing the circle back at the north. We learned that the Guardians of the Watchtowers, aka the Elemental Powers (visitors from ceremonial magic), always stand in their proper corners. (Does anyone really understand how a circle has corners?) The Powers of Elemental Earth stand in the north, those of Elemental Air stand (or waft) in the east, those of Elemental Fire stand (and flicker) in the south, and those of Elemental Water stand (or splash) in the west. Who says so?? The Received Wisdom. It's received nearly everywhere, by nearly every modern tradition, even by the Circle of Aradia—"womyn-born womyn" who are spiritual feminists and worship only the Goddess. I'm a Dianic initiate and have attended Circle of Aradia rituals where there were perhaps four hundred women present, but the circle was always cast the same old way Gerald B. Gardner (the so-called Father of Witchcraft) cast his circle: Earth, Air, Fire, Water, in that order.

**I mean no disrespect to Gardner or any priest or priestess or to any Wiccan tradition, but do we have to do it the old boys' way?**

I mean no disrespect to Gardner or any priest or priestess or to any Wiccan tradition, but do we have to do it the old boys' way? As the Received Wisdom tells us, Gardner (a retired English civil servant) came home from an overseas assignment and retired in the late 1930s. He found a home near the New Forest in southern England, where he discovered and joined the Rosicrucian Order Crotona Fellowship. Wiccan legend says he next met members of an ancient coven in the New Forest and was initiated into this coven in 1939. That's when he and his associates started inventing traditional wisdom and ancient ways of doing magic. They also started writing the books we've all read.

I'm not sure we have to plant the Elemental Powers where Gardner and his followers told them to stand. I think it makes more sense, both magically and practically, to ask the Elemental Powers to stand pretty much where they stand in the geography of the specific area where we live and work. As I've come to understand the Pagan life and the practice of magic, we live the life. We grow into it. We become grounded in both the magical life and the magic we do. That is to say, our magic becomes part of us, as much a part of us as our bones, our blood, our brain, our soul and spirit. Yes, we are grounded in our Blessed Mother Planet. She enriches each one of us, and when we come together in circle or covens, we share our connection with the natural magic of the planet. Simply put, we share how we do things.

## How to Relocate the Elements in Your Circle

So how do we learn this natural magic? How do we learn to apply it in our magical work? How do we learn where the elements stand in the circles we create?

Go outside and look around. Imagine yourself standing on the highest roof in the neighborhood. Are there mountains or forests or fields within, say, shouting distance? There's Earth. That's where your Gnomes live. Air is more abstract than Earth. How do you see Elemental Air? The winds blowing the clouds across the sky? Breezes moving the leaves on trees? Where do your prevailing winds comes from? Regular air is all around us, of course, both above and below, but is there something about the air in one direction in your neighborhood, city, or state that strikes you as somehow special? That's where your Sylphs live. Next, how do you see Elemental Fire? (As a volcano? I hope you don't live in the shadow of a volcano!) What does Elemental Fire mean to you? High energy? Loud music and dancing? Perhaps a power plant? Where do you perceive some kind of Elemental Fire?

That's where your local Salamanders play. And where is your nearest water? Do your local Undines swim in a farm pond or in a lake in a nearby park? In a swamp, a river, the closest ocean?

I've lived in Long Beach, California, on the western edge of the continent, for about twenty years. It was when I first moved here that I was inspired to go outside and look around. That's when I began rearranging my personal circle, and my changes have always worked for me. I must confess that I'm not quite sure why, but I believe that Elemental Earth is in its proper place in the north. The north seems to be "earthier," whatever that means. I feel grounded standing in the north or facing the north. To me, Elemental Fire means sunrise: bright light rising in the east and bringing fiery inspiration.

Because I live five blocks from the Pacific Ocean, at first I was sure Elemental Water occupied the west…except that Long Beach's major beach faces south. For that reason I put Elemental Water in the southern "corner" of my circle. Because the prevailing winds are westerlies where I live, we are blessed to get our Elemental Air as breezes coming inland from the Pacific. Air is my western element.

**What geographical features can you identify where you live? Carefully consider where the four Elemental Powers should most appropriately stand where you do your magic, alone or with your circle or coven.**

What geographical features can you identify where you live? Carefully consider where the four Elemental Powers should most appropriately stand where you do your magic, alone or with your circle or coven. Can you ask the local Elemental Powers to move into what are their proper directions? Try it! Cast your circle. How does it feel? The new directions might take a bit of getting used to.

One way to remember who lives where, so to speak, is to rearrange the room where your main altar is and where you do most of your personal rituals and perhaps your best meditations. Move the symbols you ordinarily keep on tables or bookshelves to other tables or shelves to mark the new stations of the Elemental Powers.

## How I Turned My Whole Home into an Altar

I've turned my living room/office into a sort of live-in altar. You can make your home or apartment a live-in altar, too. My computer is in the north under a nice window with a tree right outside. I have a huge collection of witches (350+ at last count), and the most expensive ones are standing on top of a tall bookcase against my northern wall. They "earth" me as I sit here and write. Next to my computer table stands an antique, moss-colored pot. I used to have a plant in it, but now it's about half-filled with special rocks I've collected over the years. More earthing or grounding. Some of my office supplies and the file box with my organizer supplies are also stored against the north wall. Still more grounding. My doctoral diploma and my *Llewellyn's Witches' Calendar* hang on my north wall, and, finally, against this wall stands my china cabinet, or hutch, an antique that holds precious family memorabilia, like my grandmother's cut glass cream and sugar servers. Personal grounding.

What does north mean to you? What can you move to the northern quarter of your room to make you feel more grounded and more personally filled with the power of Elemental Earth?

In my home, I find Elemental Fire (and sunrise) in the eastern wall. (Well, sure, the sun does come up in the east.) I have more witches on shelves in the east—for inspiration, to "fire me up" as I write. Hanging on the eastern wall of my office is a piece of art my brother created and gave me many years ago: it's a large tissue paper collage, all reds and oranges and yellows. I have red candles, red glass rocks, and a fat red crayon a friend once gave me on a shelf that is a small altar. Covering most of the eastern wall of my living room is a ceiling-high set of bookshelves filled with Pagan books and goddess figures, plus Kermit the Frog and a Time Dragon glass globe with Elphaba and Glinda standing in it. More inspiration, eh?

Which Elemental Power are you assigning to the east? What symbolic objects can you put along the eastern wall of your room? What symbols hold the greatest meaning to you and inspire you the most?

South means Water to me, so on the table in front of my living room's southern windows sit two or three goddesses of water, including one I bought in Glastonbury. I also once found a tiny dead crab in a garden. I brought it home and set it on a piece of white coral, which sits on a piece of sandy blue beach glass. Also on the table are some shells I've collected over the years. My TV is in the south, too. (It's where the cable is connected; sometimes we don't have a lot of choice about what must be where...but we can always adapt and add symbols.) On my TV stand sit a stuffed mermaid (pink silk body, china head and hands), a wind-up crab (which moves sideways, of course), and five or six small wind-up witches. (It's good to have a sense of humor both when you're decorating and when you're doing magic.) Finally, a stuffed witch stands next to a short blue candle, upon which I have piled half a dozen necklaces from the local Pagan Pride parades. The beads are shades of blue, the colors of water.

What does south mean to you? Which of your treasures can you move to the southern quarter of your room? How will these moves enhance your spellwork?

Finally, because the prevailing winds in Southern California are westerlies, air in my magical universe blows in from the west. On the bookshelves against my western walls are a dozen flying witches (one is part of a mobile), many birds (including an origami passenger pigeon that was part of an Audubon Society campaign many years ago), a dozen or more origami cranes, and numerous owls and Blessed Bees (see my

**This is the magic circle I live in every day. It surrounds me and everything I do at home. I didn't do all this rearranging all at once, of course, and you should also take your time. I moved a few things and evaluated the shifts in the energy.**

book *Finding New Goddesses* to learn more about the Bees). All of these magically fly through the air to shower their blessings upon me and my magic. As a bonus, on the western wall above my kitchen sink hangs a framed poster with flowers and a bee: "Bee Happy!"

This is the magic circle I live in every day. It surrounds me and everything I do at home. I didn't do all this rearranging all at once, of course, and you should also take your time. I moved a few things and evaluated the shifts in the energy. Sometimes I put something back where it had been. I still keep checking on the energy, especially when I do a new ritual.

## Think Carefully about Where You Move Your Elemental Symbols

You likewise don't have to immediately rearrange your whole life and suddenly discombobulate whoever lives with you. Think about what you can do. Make some sketches. Talk to other Pagans and Witches. Take it one step at a time. After you've made your first shift, focus on the energy. What has changed? What's feeling better? Can you move any of your smaller altars to other parts of the room? How will that work? When you've created your personal live-in magic circle, what important souvenirs of your life will be in which direction? Can you already feel what the energy will be? Can you sense how happy and content you will be living "in" an altar?

An important note: When we go to public rituals or rituals in other people's homes, it would, of course, be highly rude to insist that they move their elements around just to satisfy us. I always adjust myself to their circle and settle into how the magic moves. You should do that, too. In all my years as a Witch, I've experienced almost no cognitive dissonance between my personal magic circle and any public circle I've stood in. We can all go with the flow of any ritual. Use your best and clearest vision to focus on the energies, no matter in which direction they're flowing. And, again, go with that flow. Add your own best wisdom to the Received Wisdom.

**Barbara Ardinger, PhD** *(English—mostly Shakespeare), has been writing for the Llewellyn annuals since 2004. Her work has also been published in devotionals to* Isis, Athena, *and* Brigid. *She is the author of* Secret Lives, *a novel about crones and other magical folk, and* Pagan Every Day, *a unique daybook of daily meditations. Her other books include* Goddess Meditations *(the first-ever book—published by* Llewellyn*—of meditations focusing solely on goddesses) and* Finding New Goddesses *(a parody of goddess encyclopedias). Her blogs and/or stories appear every month on* Feminism & Religion, *https://feminismandreligion.com, where she is a regular Pagan contributor. She lives in* Long Beach, *California, with Schroedinger, her rescued calico cat.*

**Illustrator: Bri Hermanson**

# Is Negative Energy More Powerful Than Good?

*Mortellus*

Sometimes a question shows up in your inbox and it seems so incredibly straightforward that you immediately hit reply, only to find the cursor blinking in front of you. When I was first asked the seemingly straightforward question "Is negative energy (or magic) more powerful than good?" I truly thought it would be a simple thing to express my opinion. But it wasn't, and as the cursor continued to blink in front of me—I found myself confronted with more questions than answers. What is energy? What defines

"negative" or "positive" energy/magic? What is power? I grappled with wanting to simply state that, no, it isn't, but neither does the inverse hold true. That not only does the universe need a balance, but I don't believe there's any such thing as "negative" or "positive," that the answer is as easy as determining who you are and what your intention is.

But I realized almost immediately that at least in terms of the question at hand, I was wrong. I have always believed that magic—and, for the topic at hand, "energy"—is a force comparable to electricity. Neither good nor bad, electricity can power your reading lamp just the same as it can power an electric chair. What matters, of course, is who's throwing the switch; but electricity does possess "positives" and "negatives." For as much as I'd railed against the idea of "white" or "black" magic, I was still putting intention (as a magical concept) into a similar box, while ignoring that magic, just like electricity, isn't without positives and negatives.

## Positives and Negatives

In my writing, I've often equated the underworld to the zero-point energy field, the incorporeal dead to dark matter, and reincarnation to the law of conservation of energy (which says that energy can neither be created nor destroyed; it can only take another form); and, well, I find myself yet again poking about in quantum physics looking for answers. Energy in the context of magical practice might be equated to the aforementioned positive and negative electric charges; when speaking of electricity, we understand that like (or same) charges repel one another, and, as the old idiom goes, unlike (or opposite) charges attract. Positive charges, always repelling, push outward—a burst of energy like the big bang…ever growing larger; negative charges, forever attracting, pull inward, like death itself drawing us to our inevitable end.

## Does Positive Equate to Goodness?

When it comes to magical energy, we tend to look at positive workings as benignant: aligned with life and creation, that big bang perhaps, the right hand, the physical plane, and living beings. Negative workings, on the other (left) hand, are seemingly malefic, aligned with death and destruction, the ethereal plane, and the dead. As someone who primarily works with death as an energetic force, I've often been troubled by this perception of negatively charged magic, and the harmful stereotyping that comes along with it. Death magic (necromancy), it seems, is perceived to be not only powerful, but evil, and other.

Instinctively we believe that whether it be magic or physics, energy must always be positive; positivity means creation, existence, mass—goodness—and negative energy is, well, the absence of all of those things (Grumiller, Parekh, and Riegler 2019). It represents a nothingness, and we want to believe that the amount of energy in the universe is always greater than nothing, that it is *positive*—everywhere, all the time (Aigner et al. 2019). We want this to be true—we *need* it to be true—otherwise formulas like $E = mc^2$ become broken; negative energy would mean negative mass, which means, well, gravity doesn't work anymore (Ford and Roman 1999). We don't want to believe that we can extract energy, mass, or creation from nothingness; nor do we wish to believe that positive magical energy could be derived from a negatively charged source, because to do so is to owe the universe itself a debt.

## Quantum Interest

If the dead, the underworld, and even negative and, by necessity, positive magical energy, as I propose, are all simply quantum states with energy/mass or the lack thereof, then they are also by necessity entangled with quantum interest (Ford and Roman 1999). Quantum physics, time and again, contradicts our instincts and intuitions. It tells us that, yes, we can borrow energy from nothingness, find creation in destruction—life in death—utilize negative energy, but there is a limit. The quantum interest conjecture states that not only does nature allow for negative energy, it accounts for it as part of the equation, and does so without violating the law of conservation of energy (Ford and Roman 1999). Why? Because for negative energy to even begin to flow from a particular source, compensating positive energy must flow from that same place, at that same time (Ford and Roman 1999).

Though the outcome might be complicated by the borrowing, the universe does not let us take from nothing. Even as all living things must one day die, positive energy can become negatively charged; and as all things dead create life or perhaps go on to live again, negative energy can become positively charged (Grumiller, Parekh, and Riegler 2019). These bonds of positive and negative, entangled on a quantum scale, prove to us beyond a shadow of a doubt that negative energy cannot be more powerful than good, nor can we assign more power to goodness, because the universe in its wisdom simply will not allow one to exist without the other.

## Is Our Perspective Broken?

Sometimes it seems that as magical practitioners we want to divide magic itself down the middle and call it one thing or another; but the universe is not black and white, and it is never that simple. We occupy a universe with a rainbow of emotions, people, beliefs, actions, and, yes, even "kinds" of magic. Our magic simply cannot function fully and honestly if kept in a monochromatic box where some things are right and some are wrong, some are positive and some are negative. It just doesn't work that way; like life and death itself, positive and negative share an indelible bond.

## Positive Negative Asymmetry

While trying to understand why that might be, I stumbled upon a psychological phenomenon known as positive negative asymmetry. It means, basically, that we humans are likely to recall an insult with more clarity than a compliment, or a slight better than a kindness. It means that one adverse event will ensure that we refer to an otherwise wonderful day as "bad" if asked how it was (Lewicka, Czapinski, and Peeters 1992). Studies have shown that we perceive negative information as more truthful, and I wonder if we are playing out those same biases in our magic (Hilbig 2012). Do we believe, deep in our subconscious mind, that "negative" energy is more honest (Peeters and Czapinski 1990)? Is this why we are more inclined to believe in a curse than a boon, and what does it mean in terms of how we perceive the power of negatively charged magic as opposed to its positively charged kin? Is it simply that we need something that we might declare "bad" but powerful so that our struggles seem outside our control? When we fail to succeed because we live in an often cruel and chaotic world, is it easier to say that it is because we are unwilling to do magic that we perceive as powerful but evil?

## Living in Balance

Here are some tips for finding that necessary balance between negatively and positively charged magic in your own practice:

- Consider magic not as a binary of good/bad, active/passive, or black/white, but instead as the poles of a magnet or positive and negative electric charges.
- Assign the qualities of Life and Death to Goddess and God (where applicable), meditating on that as a polarity outside of outdated and harmful constructs such as "feminine and masculine," "passive and active," and so on.

- Replace constructs such as "negative and positive" or "baneful/ malefic and benignant" with Life and Death. Consider their energetic qualities like positive and negative electric charges—pushing and pulling, creating and destroying.
- As always, my best advice is to be wary of advice. Listen to your own heart, and determine where you stand on issues rather than parroting harmful stereotypes. Let us live in balance not just with our magic, but with one another.

## Bibliography

Aigner, Florian, and Vienna University of Technology. "Quantum Vacuum: Negative Energy & Repulsive Gravity." SciTechDaily, October 2, 2019. Accessed March 7, 2022. https://scitechdaily.com/quantum-vacuum-negative-energy-repulsive-gravity/.

Ford, L. H., and Thomas A. Roman. "The Quantum Interest Conjecture." *Physical Review D* 60, no. 10 (October 22, 1999). Accessed March 7, 2022. https://doi.org/10.1103/physrevd.60.104018.

Grumiller, Daniel, Pulastya Parekh, and Max Riegler. "Local Quantum Energy Conditions in Non-Lorentz-Invariant Quantum Field Theories." *Physical Review Letters* 123, no. 12 (September 20, 2019). Accessed March 7, 2022. https://doi.org/10.1103/physrevlett.123.121602.

Hilbig, Benjamin E. "Good Things Don't Come Easy (to Mind)." *Experimental Psychology* 59, no. 1 (January 1, 2011): 38–46. Accessed March 7, 2022. https://doi.org/10.1027/1618-3169/a000124.

Hooft, Gerard. "Ontology in Quantum Mechanics" In *Topics on Quantum Information Science*, edited by Sergio Curilef and Angel Ricardo Plastino. London: IntechOpen, 2021. Accessed March 7, 2022. DOI: 10.5772/intechopen.99852.

Jones, W. Paul. "Death as a Factor in Understanding Modern Attitudes Toward the Aging." *Journal of Religion & Aging* 3, no. 1–2 (September 14, 1987): 75–90. Accessed March 7, 2022. https://doi.org/10.1300/j491v03n01_07.

Kaplan, Hasan. "Belief in a Just World, Religiosity and Victim Blaming." *Archive for the Psychology of Religion* 34, no. 3 (September 2012): 397–409. Accessed March 7, 2022. https://doi.org/10.1163/15736121-12341246.

LeDoux, J. E., J. Moscarello, R. Sears, and V. Campese. "The Birth, Death and Resurrection of Avoidance: A Reconceptualization of a Troubled Paradigm." *Molecular Psychiatry* 22, no. 1 (October 18, 2016): 24–36. Accessed March 7, 2022. https://doi.org/10.1038/mp.2016.166.

Lewicka, Maria, Janusz Czapinski, and Guido Peeters. "Positive-Negative Asymmetry or 'When the Heart Needs a Reason.'" *European Journal of Social Psychology* 22, no. 5 (September 1992): 425–34. Accessed March 7, 2022. https://doi.org/10.1002/ejsp.2420220502.

Peeters, Guido, and Janusz Czapinski. "Positive-Negative Asymmetry in Evaluations: The Distinction Between Affective and Informational Negativity Effects." *European Review of Social Psychology* 1, no. 1 (January 1990): 33–60. Accessed March 7, 2022. https://doi.org/10.1080/14792779108401856.

Solomon, Sheldon, Jeff Greenberg, and Thomas A Pyszczynski. *The Worm at the Core: On the Role of Death in Life*. London: Penguin Books, 2016.

**Mortellus** *is the High Priestex of the Coven of Leaves, a Gardnerian coven operating an Outer Court training group who like to say that they are a bubbling cauldron of bitter esoterica slithering their way through Western North Carolina. Additionally, Mortellus is a mortician, medium, and necromancer, and the author of* Do I Have To Wear Black? Rituals, Customs & Funerary Etiquette for Modern Pagans. *Currently, they reside on three acres that are hastily becoming overgrown again with their spouse, three-year-old twins, and one really, really ridiculous dog.*

**Illustrator: M. Kathryn Thompson**

# Magical Self-Care

## Nurture Your Body, Mind & Spirit

# Witchy Workouts

Autumn Damiana

*Ugh*, I think to myself for the hundredth time after passing a mirror. It's 2021 and I've been mostly sedentary for the last year and a half, and I can't help but notice how much rounder and flabbier I've become. The COVID-19 pandemic forced most people inside for many months, and conservative estimates claim that the average person gained somewhere between fifteen and twenty pounds during this time period. I am certainly no exception, and it shows. My weight and fitness level have definitely suffered, and I need to get back in shape.

Starting a new workout regimen is hard, so I've decided that this time I am going to do it the witchy way. I will, of course, do the physical work required, but I will also use magic and spellcraft to help me along. Any Witch can similarly apply their talents to reach their fitness goals.

First, you need to ask yourself why you want to work out. Maybe you want to lose weight or get better sleep, or perhaps your doctor recommended it. Maybe you have multiple reasons. I personally hope to drop some pounds, but I also want to manage my stress levels and treat my dog to some longer walks and hikes. If you want to start working out or need help motivating yourself to keep going, think about *all* the reasons you should do it, not just one. What if eventually you want to learn a new sport, train for a marathon, boost your immune system, or lower your blood pressure? I make this point because if you want to use Witchcraft to achieve your goals, it is exponentially helpful if you can apply it on multiple levels.

## Keep a Workout Journal

Whether you are an exercise newbie or a seasoned pro, the first place to start a witchy workout is with a journal. Writing in a journal is a way to give yourself guidance by recording your successes and failures and jotting down ideas, questions, feelings, and strategies. This will keep you motivated and on track, help you monitor your progress, and allow you the space to problem-solve. Think of it as a Book of Shadows for your fitness quest. Before I started a witchy workout, I kept a food journal where I recorded what I ate and how many calories I consumed and sometimes included a brief entry about what was going on that day or in my life in general. I learned so much about myself from just that small amount of information! Here are some journal prompt examples with a witchy focus to get you started writing:

1. Daily affirmations or mantras: "I believe in myself" or "I am healthier today than I was yesterday." These are words of power and should inspire you.
2. Words of gratitude: "I'm so happy I saw that sunset during my jog" or "I give thanks that I can afford nutritious food."
3. Magical meals: Use a versatile recipe where you can pick and choose ingredients based on their magical correspondences. Examples include smoothies, soups, stir-fries, and quiches.
4. Write a prayer to a deity: "I thank you, Aphrodite, for the beautiful body I have been given. Please help me to love myself as I am."
5. Make a mini vision board: Draw a representation of yourself in the middle of the page, then sketch all the things you would like to attract around you. Use symbols to keep it simple. Use an hourglass for slimming down, a calendar with a date depicted of an event for which you want to get fit, a leaf for growth, a barbell for strength, etc. Draw large, exaggerated arrows from each symbol pointed toward the drawing of you. Visualize each of these things coming into your life.
6. Daily tarot card (or other oracle card) reading: Pick one card right after you get up to give you guidance and insight into your workout for that day.
7. Create a magical sigil defining your fitness goals, then inscribe it at the top of every page.
8. List a helpful witchy website: How are you using this information in your workout? One that I use is mountainroseherbs.com. They have a variety of wellness products, like essential oils, tea blends, and natural bath and body supplies. Their blog and podcasts are also full of healthy herbal tips and recipes.

9. Spells! Your spellcraft should always be written down so you can decide what is successful and what you need to tweak in the future. Try the weight loss spell later in this article to get you started.
10. Make a batch of crystal infusion water using the instructions in the next section. Record exactly what you did and how you made it along with your results.

## Workout Chants

One of the main gripes I have with exercising is that it is boring and repetitive, and my mind tends to wander aimlessly as I go through the motions. So I've decided that one way to make the most of my workout would be to chant or sing in my mind, focusing my intent and building positive energy using the power I generate through the movements of my body, which I release at the end of my workout before I cool down—like casting a spell. This is perfect for walking, jogging, running, biking, weight lifting, or any other repetitive motion. The chants can be used with music, and the song lyrics are set to nursery rhymes or folk songs. You can also make up your own—it doesn't matter how silly they are, as long as they are memorable and state what you want to achieve. Here are a few chants that I like to use:

1. General workout chant:

*One, two, three, four: steady, just a little more!*
*Five, six, seven, eight: looking good and feeling great!*

2. Better health chant:

*One, two, three, four: vitality will be restored!*
*Five, six, seven, eight: all my cells rejuvenate!*

3. Chant to push yourself harder:

*One, two, three, four:* I *am ruthless, hear me roar!*
*Five, six, seven, eight: on this track* I *dominate!*
(Or use whatever you are exercising on, such as "bike," "trail," or "mill" for "treadmill.")

4. Inspirational chant:

*Eight, seven, six, five: it feels so good to be alive!*
*Four, three, two, one: working out is so much fun!*

5. Motivational chant:

*Eight, seven, six, five:* I *have the will,* I *have the drive!*
*Four, three, two, one: before* I *know it, I'll be done!*

6. Chant sung to "My Bonnie Lies Over the Ocean":

*My body is full of motion, my body belongs to me;*
*My body is full of motion, and healthy my body will be!*

7. Chant sung to "Happy Birthday":

*Happy workout for me, I'm working hard as can be!*
*Happy workout, then I'll chill out, happy workout for me!*

## Crystal Infusion Water

That first gulp of cool, clear, refreshing water after a workout can be pure bliss. Take it to the next level by infusing the water with crystals that align with your magical intent. When you drink crystal infusion water, you are consuming the essence of the stone and its magical properties. You can also drink some prior to or during your workout to enhance your routine. Here is a short guide that explains how to make and use these enchanting elixirs.

First, a quick word about safety. Many crystals react badly to water, and many others are toxic. Some stones contain high amounts of aluminum, asbestos, lead, copper, or even small levels of radiation. If in doubt, err on the side of caution and *do not* submerge the stone in water that you are planning to drink. To be on the safe side, you can use stones that are part of the quartz family. Quartz is one of the hardest, most common, and most stable of all crystalline structures. Here is a list of safe stones to use in your drinking water:

**Clear Quartz:** This is an all-purpose stone that can be programmed with any intent. It is also wonderful to use if you simply need a little support, as it will amplify any other magical working.

**Amethyst:** Use this crystal for help with addictions. If you binge eat or drink, smoke, or use drugs, or if you engage in obsessive behavior like weighing or judging yourself too much, this is the stone for you.

**Rose Quartz:** The ultimate stone of self-love, rose quartz is the go-to for building a positive body image. Use it when you want to develop a healthier emotional relationship with your body or need help seeing your beauty and potential.

**Tiger's-Eye:** If you need energy and focus, use tiger's-eye. This stone will give you the push you need to fully commit to your workout regimen.

**Aventurine:** This stone is green, the color of healing and growth. As a "lucky" crystal, aventurine can be used for any kind of physical therapy and/or to help you reach your workout goals.

**Red Jasper:** This stone works well for lending strength. If you are weight training or trying to build muscle or endurance, you can use red jasper to assist you.

**Blue Agate:** This is the perfect cool down stone and is also good for soothing a tired spirit. Call on blue agate when you need to ramp down after a particularly intense workout.

**Citrine:** This is the "happy" crystal. It neutralizes negativity and replaces it with joy and enthusiasm. Use citrine whenever you need some encouragement or motivation or just want to celebrate your accomplishments.

Cleanse your crystal physically and energetically at the same time. Scrub it with dish soap using a toothbrush, and rinse thoroughly. Then ring a bell or singing bowl over the crystal. (You can also use a tuning fork or chime.) The next step is to charge it with your intent. Hold the crystal and tap on it gently with your finger, like you would poke someone to get their attention. Then put it near your mouth and speak into it:

*Awaken,* (*name of crystal*). *I charge you with the powers of* (*purpose*). *Please give me* (*your magical intention*). *So mote it be.*

Here is an example:

*Awaken,* Red Jasper. *I charge you with the powers of endurance. Please give me extra stamina during my routine today. So mote it be.*

Place your crystal(s) into a glass or pitcher of water. Let the stones infuse for at least three to four hours. You can also put them in the refrigerator overnight. When you are ready to drink your crystal infusion water, remove the stones and drink or pour your water into a bottle to enjoy later, during or after your workout. For best results, you should make, store, and drink your crystal infusion water in glass vessels and containers if possible.

## Weight Loss Cleansing Spell

This is a two-part spell, so plan accordingly. It is meant to jump-start your weight loss or give you a much-needed breakthrough if you start to plateau.

Materials needed:

- A white candle in a holder
- A pin or small knife
- A bay leaf
- A small glass jar with a top or a cork
- Skin-safe oil (Almond, avocado, coconut, or even olive or vegetable oil will work.)
- Essential oils (optional)
- An eyebrow pencil or pencil eyeliner (You can find these at most dollar stores.)
- A bath sponge or loofah (optional)

### Part 1: Prepare Your Ingredients

Do this during any of the three days of a full moon. Take the white candle and use the pin or knife to carve these words into it: "health" on one side and "weight loss" on the other side. Then add the bay leaf to the jar and pour a quarter cup or more of oil into it. Add a few drops of essential oils if you like. Use rose, lavender, sandalwood, patchouli, or whatever scent makes you feel gorgeous and attractive. Seal the jar and shake it. Cup it in your hands and visualize yourself healthier and losing weight. Place the jar where the light of the full moon will shine on it overnight. Save the oil for the second part of the spell.

### Part 2: The Weight Loss Cleansing

This can be done any day of the waning moon. Take the eyebrow pencil and draw circles around the areas of your body where you want to lose weight, like the stomach, love handles, thighs, etc. Dress your candle with the charged oil. Light the candle in its holder and place it in your bathroom. Turn out all the lights and use this candle for illumination. (You can also light other candles if you wish.) Pour a small amount of oil into the palms of your hands. Rub the oil on the circles you have drawn on yourself until the lines blur and become no more than dirty smudges, using more oil as needed. As you do this, chant these words:

> *By herb and oil, wax and wick,*
> *and waning moon, I lose weight quick!*

Then get in the shower, soap up, and scrub yourself with a sponge or loofah if needed, rinsing everything down the drain. Keep up your workout routine and repeat this spell if necessary every full moon cycle until you reach your desired weight.

**Autumn Damiana** *is an author, artist, crafter, and amateur photographer. She is a solitary eclectic* Cottage Witch *who has been following her* Pagan *path for almost two decades and is a regular contributor to the* Llewellyn *annuals. Along with writing and making art,* Autumn *has a degree in early childhood education and is currently pursuing further studies. She lives with her husband and doggie familiar in the beautiful* San Francisco Bay Area. *Visit her online at autumndamiana.com.*

**Illustrator: M. Kathryn Thompson**

# The Magic of Self-Care: Being Present for Your Own Life

*Gwion Raven*

So much of our witchcraft focuses on the things we do, what we create, what we manifest into being, and how we celebrate the sabbats. It's all about checking off the next item on our witchy to-do list—memorize the songs, learn to read tarot, study herb lore, write the perfect ritual, start a coven, and so on. What if our initial magical training included thirty days of self-care, or—let's be real—thirty minutes of self-care? What if part of our magical practice became "what I shall not do today" rather than "magical techniques that can I master today"?

I always thought my practice had a lot of self-care built into it, but the more I examined what I do each day and each month, the more I realized it doesn't. And here's the revelation that blew my mind: When I don't practice great self-care, I can't do magic. Not even a little bit! I suspect if you talk with my family, friends, covenmates, and coworkers, they'd probably tell you I'm not particularly good at much of anything when I don't make a concerted effort to make time for self-care. There's a direct relationship between my ability to focus on magic and my ability to take care of my physical, mental, and spiritual health. It turns out I'm a much less effective magic worker when I am stressed-out, not paying attention to the signals my body is sending me, and continually exposing myself to information and situations that are deleterious to my overall well-being.

**I'm not particularly good at much of anything when I don't make a concerted effort to make time for self-care. There's a direct relationship between my ability to focus on magic and my ability to take care of my physical, mental, and spiritual health.**

So what's a witch to do? In my case, I had to seriously dig in and understand what self-care is and what it is not.

## What Self-Care Isn't

A common misconception about self-care is that it is just another term for self-pampering. Many people believe that self-care is all about getting massages every now and again, or taking a long bath, or binge-watching your favourite show whilst eating a whole box of crackers and polishing off an entire block of really good cheese. (No judgment here! I unapologetically do all of these occasionally.) And while it's true that going for massages, enjoying a relaxing bath, and indulging in spectacularly good cheese every so often are all pretty fantastic and can contribute to your overall well-being, they are only small parts of what a self-care regimen really entails.

Another phrase thrown around that's often mistaken for a synonym of self-care is spoiling yourself. If you're anything like me, when I hear this phrase, I'm instantly transported back to being a child and being told how spoiled I was if I asked for anything. As an adult, the idea of spoiling myself became conflated with being selfish, frivolously wasting time, and engaging in activities that I should feel guilty about. There is a pernicious notion that when we spend time, money, or resources on taking care of our own needs, we're either depriving another person of happiness or focusing on ourselves undeservedly.

Just to be super clear, though, you absolutely should pamper and spoil yourself whenever possible to the best of your ability. If pampering yourself involves other people, there are three key things to consider: full and enthusiastic consent from everyone involved, showing your heartfelt appreciation, and tipping well!

The last incorrect definition of self-care I'll give you here is any version that connotes weakness on your part. There's this myth out there that we are superhuman beings who can work sixty hours a week, always stay on top of running our homes, maintain perfect health, perform magical work for others on demand, and never require any time off to rest and recharge. If you've ever taken a day off to reset or requested downtime or told a partner that you just can't today, congratulations! There's nothing wrong with that. In fact, you should probably do it more often than you think. We are not machines. We are not perpetual workers. Our bodies, minds, and spirits demand attention. Resting is not a sign of weakness. Illness is not tantamount

to laziness. Stopping for the sake of stopping is part of being a human. Self-care is not you wimping out on life. Stopping once in a while is actually a requirement.

## What Self-Care Is

Now that we know what self-care isn't, let's define just what it is. Self-care means consciously engaging in actions that encourage and support your overall well-being. Having a self-care practice includes activities that you enjoy doing because they bring you some measure of relaxation, peace, balance, or rest. The key to self-care is that you participate in your self-care practice on a regular and consistent basis. Self-care encompasses your entire environment and virtually every aspect of your life, from having a level of financial stability to making space for rest, having fun, eating in a way that supports your body's needs, accessing appropriate health care, finding avenues for emotional support, and cultivating safe and secure spaces to live and work in. That's a lot different from just getting a massage or eating a decadent dessert, right?

**Self-care means consciously engaging in actions that encourage and support your overall well-being. Having a self-care practice includes activities that you enjoy doing because they bring you some measure of relaxation, peace, balance, or rest.**

Let me ask you a question. If you could wave a magic wand right now and instantly feel more content, reduce the amount of daily stress piled up on your shoulders, and be generally more at peace with your life situation, would you cast that spell? Answer honestly here. Don't get caught up in overthinking your magical process or the potential consequences. What does your gut say? Less stress, more happiness. Yes or no?

What did you answer?

Notice that you weren't asked to wave a magic wand to make all your troubles go away. Self-care isn't a wish-fulfilling spell that shows you how to find the gold coin at the bottom of a giant pile of horse poop. A self-care practice won't suddenly fill your bank account, erase past pain, or restore you to perfect health overnight (or maybe ever). Also notice that nowhere in the definition of self-care is there any mention of saving the planet or raising awareness about ________ (fill in the cause you are passionate about). Doing that kind of work is needed, should be applauded, and hopefully one day will make a huge impact on the lives of a great number of people. But you can *totally stop doing it for thirty minutes a day or take the weekend off and recharge yourself.* A burned-out activist, social worker, magic worker, or human being is no real help to the revolution, whichever revolution you'd like to see.

## Making Self-Care a Priority

I'm a busy witch. I own my own business, co-own a metaphysical shop, teach workshops, write books, and work locally within a couple thriving magical traditions. There's plenty of other stuff to fill up my days too, like making meals, taking out the garbage, walking the dog, tending my garden, paying bills, being a husband, being a father to adult children, and worrying about the state of the world. Whilst the specifics might be different, I'm guessing your life is packed to bursting with an endless list of tasks to complete every day as well.

If you look over my list, you can see there's not a lot of time left for me to take care of me. When I'm doing a thousand things and managing projects and being responsible to or for other people, I become a bit of a nonfactor in the equation. That's when the trouble starts for me.

I quickly go down the path of resenting everything I'm doing for others and then I push off work and then I get on the shame train, telling myself I'm a failure and no good for anything. That's a sure road to depression, which is a condition I've struggled with for years. When life gets on top of me and I have way too much going on, it shows up in missed deadlines, unreturned emails, ignored voicemails, and a total lack of being able to do any kind of effective magic.

So I changed the way I do life. Maybe it's more accurate to say I'm changing the way I'm doing life, because it is an ever-evolving practice. I've developed a self-care and magical practice that begins with making me the main priority in my life. That's not to say I don't consider other people or shirk my responsibilities; I've just reorganized what I do each day, identified the conditions in which I will say yes to adding something, and learned to set better boundaries when I have to say no to someone. The result is that I have more time to relax and make space for myself, even if that's just for five minutes.

## Self-Care Spell

Okay! It's time to do a little magic to help you with your self-care practice. Most magically inclined people believe in some form of the phrase words have power. We also know that if we set an intention, fix our will on a specific outcome, and work magic to support what we're focusing on, it's much more likely to come to fruition. That's what we're going to do now with this piece of magic. Create the time and space to do magic for at least thirty minutes by yourself. You can totally do this working with someone else later, but the first time you do it, it's just for you. Here's what you'll need:

- A biggish piece of paper (like from a notebook)
- A bunch of smallish pieces of paper (like yellow sticky notes)

- Something to write with
- Two bowls—one should be fireproof (like a cast-iron cauldron)
- A pair of scissors
- Matches or a lighter

Once you've gathered everything, make your space magical. You can cast a circle, light candles, put on your favourite piece of witchy music, wear your best ritual clothes, invoke your magical guides and allies, or whatever you do to get ready to make magic.

On the large piece of paper, write everything you did today. Everything—woke up, brushed my teeth, checked social media, ate a great breakfast, called my mum, dropped the kids off, took my medications, spent eight hours serving customers, spent sixty minutes fighting traffic to get home, made out with my partner(s), pet my cat for ten minutes. You get the idea. Write as much as you possibly can remember from your day.

Now get seven of the smaller pieces of paper and write out the following categories, one category per sticky note:

- This supports me emotionally
- This supports my physical well-being
- This makes me happy
- This lowers my stress or anxiety
- This connects me to magic, the gods, my craft, the divine, the world
- I love, love, love doing this
- All the other stuff I did today that doesn't fit into these categories

Spread the sticky notes with the seven categories out around you. Look at the list you wrote of everything you did today. Write each item on that list on a sticky note and place it under the sticky note with the most appropriate category. If some activities feel like they fit in a couple of places, you can write them more than once. Be relentlessly honest with yourself.

How much of your day was spent doing what you love, love, love? How much of your time was spent engaging in activities that support your well-being? Are there more items in the "All the other stuff" category than in the "This makes me happy" pile? There will always be things you must do that you'd rather not do but are necessary for your life to work. But is there a way to rearrange your day so you are doing more of what helps you connect with the world and makes you happy?

If there are categories with very few activities listed, grab more sticky notes and fill each section with stuff that you do love to do and is supportive of your well-being. Save this new list somewhere. Take a picture of it. Keep it on your phone or your fridge or email it to yourself. Look at this list regularly and keep finding ways to fill the moments of your day with what you want to be doing.

In this working, in this place of magic between worlds, remove any activities that don't support your vision of self-care, especially if they are harmful to you. Maybe they can't go away entirely, but can you deprioritize them? Put them in the fireproof bowl and burn them as a symbol that you're transforming them, releasing them. (You can absolutely choose not to burn items and opt to compost or recycle them instead. Magical safety tip: If you do burn something, never leave it unattended and always have a way to extinguish it close at hand.)

Close this spell by speaking out loud everything you've written that brings you joy, happiness, support, connection, etc. Recite each thing at least three times. Make it a chant, shout it out loudly for the world to hear, or whisper it so only you can hear it, but do say it. Thank yourself for making time to complete this spell.

There you have it. You have combined your magic with your desire to have a better relationship with your self-care practice. You've identified what you want to do and what you want to do less of. By the way, if you doubt how effective a spell like this can be, consider that if you performed this magical working, you found thirty minutes to do magic for yourself, by yourself. The spell is already working. Keep at it!

**Gwion Raven** *is a tattooed Pagan, writer, traveler, musician, cook, kitchen witch, occult shop owner, and teacher, and the author of* The Magick of Food: Rituals, Offerings & Why We Eat Together *and* Life Ritualized: A Witch's Guide to Honoring Life's Important Moments. *Although initiated in three magickal traditions, Gwion describes his practice as virtually anything that celebrates the wild, sensuous, living, breathing, dancing, ecstatic, divine experiences of this lifetime. Born and raised in London, he now resides in Northern California and shares space with redwood trees, the Pacific Ocean, and his beloved partner. Visit Gwion at GwionRaven.com and on Instagram @themagickoffood.*

**Illustrator: Tim Foley**

# Essential Self-Care Rituals for Sensitive People

*Tess Whitehurst*

Magical people are sensitive people. We feel a lot. We don't just *see* nature; we *feel* nature. We don't just *hear* music; we *feel* music. And we don't just notice how other people are feeling; we often feel their feelings too.

Your sensitivity is a gift: it makes it possible for you to live your life fully, perceive beauty deeply, and tune in to psychic and intuitive information that other people might miss. But without proper self-care, your sensitivity can also be a burden. It can overwhelm you, distract you, and make it difficult to separate yourself from any stress and negativity

that may be floating around in interior spaces, group settings, and the culture at large. Your sensitivity, when not properly managed, can even cause you to disconnect or disengage, which can negatively affect your magic, relationships, and mental health.

That's why it's important to take care of yourself properly so you can wield your sensitivity with wisdom, mastery, and grace. Here are some essential practices that will help you do that.

## Daily Magical Hygiene Practice

As a sensitive magical person, I cannot overstress the importance of attending to your magical hygiene daily. To keep your energy balanced and harmonious, it's ideal to make your magical hygiene practice as important as taking a shower and brushing your teeth.

Here's a simple magical hygiene practice you can try. Feel free to use it as a template to craft your own version. While this is a great place to start, over time you can allow your own personal practice to shift and change until you discover what works best for you.

To begin, sit on a meditation cushion, perhaps in front of your altar or somewhere else where you won't be disturbed. You can also sit in a chair or on a couch if that's more comfortable for you. Just be sure to keep your back straight in an alert, relaxed way.

Take three long, deep breaths. Extend them for as long as you comfortably can. Then allow your breathing to be natural, and simply place your attention on it. Notice as you breathe in and out. As you do this, you'll be amazed at how quickly your breathing begins to deepen all on its own. You will also notice areas of tension in your body, which you can imagine you are breathing air into. Over time, you'll begin to notice the feeling of energy moving all throughout your body as if propelled by the breath.

When you feel grounded and centered, imagine yourself as light. Feel the energetic aliveness of your body, and see if you can sense it as bright white-gold light. Sense your body as light and the energy around your body—your aura—as light. In your mind's eye, see and sense yourself as a sphere of blindingly bright light that looks like the sun.

Now extend your light downward into the earth, like a root or a pillar. Sense it moving down quickly and naturally until it enters into the center of the earth. See or imagine the center of the earth as another sphere of bright light, like an underground sun. Connect your personal light to this golden light at the center of the earth. Sense this earth light moving upward into your aura and body, refreshing and brightening your own personal sphere. It's as if you are a cell phone and you're being plugged into an outlet in order to recharge.

Next, send your light upward from the crown of your head, as if it's a trunk or a pillar of light. See it moving up and up until it exits the earth's atmosphere. Imagine that at the center of the universe there's a giant cosmic sun. Continue sending your light upward until it enters the very center of this sun. Then sense this light moving down the trunk or pillar and entering your own personal sphere. Once again, allow yourself to recharge.

Breathe now and feel light moving up from the center of the earth and down from the center of the infinite cosmic sun. Allow yourself to heal deeply in whatever ways you need to. Remember that you can always draw upon these earthly and infinite sources, so you need never feel depleted or drained.

Set the clear intention that only love may enter your own personal sphere of light. You may perceive other energies, and they may be in your vicinity, but the bright light around and within you will purify them so that you can see and interact with other people and the world from a place of love.

## Elemental Energy Healing Ritual

This is one of my favorite self-care rituals to do because it never fails to significantly boost the way I feel on all levels: physical, emotional, mental, and spiritual. It's so simple and so reliable. I like to do it as much as possible, but I'm especially likely to do it when I feel stressed, overwhelmed, low on energy, or in any way out of whack. It's grounding and uplifting and it brings your personal energy into a state of harmonious equilibrium. You can do it for as long as you want, but it only needs to take five minutes or so. I recommend doing it as frequently as you can.

**I like to do it as much as possible, but I'm especially likely to do it when I feel stressed, overwhelmed, low on energy, or in any way out of whack. It's grounding and uplifting and it brings your personal energy into a state of harmonious equilibrium.**

Be aware that getting outside for this ritual can often be the hardest part. Perhaps because we spend so much of our time indoors, making the jump from inside to out can often seem harder or less worth it than it actually is. It's almost as if the more you need this ritual, the more daunting it becomes in your mind to step out of the door. But just by knowing about this little mental hurdle, you can more easily overcome it. Push through your resistance and walk out of the door, and the rest will be much easier and much more inspiring, uplifting, and healing than you expected. (I know this from experience.)

Visit a body of water. If you're in a city or a desert area and you can't get to a beach, lake, river, or stream, even a canal or outdoor fountain will be great. If it's winter and everything is frozen, a frozen body of water or even snow on the ground will also work.

Sit or stand comfortably near the water and gaze at it. Simply appreciate its sound and/or appearance. Begin to notice the other forms of beauty that surround you, such as clouds, birds, sunlight, and plants.

Once you feel calm and present, look in your immediate surroundings for a representation of the earth element: a rock, a plant, a tree, dirt, sand, or even a flat expanse of sidewalk or street. As you look at and connect with this earthly representation, think to yourself, "Earth, earth, earth, earth…"

Now look for a representation of the air element: clouds, birds, a butterfly, or wind through the trees. As you enjoy being present with this representation of air, think to yourself, "Air, air, air, air…"

Next, if it's daytime, become aware of the sun. (Of course, don't stare at it directly.) If the sun is behind a cloud, notice the light it still provides. And if it's nighttime, become aware of the stars. If it's cloudy, see if you can still get in touch with their sparkling presence in the vast distance. Think to yourself, "Fire, fire, fire, fire…"

Now it's time to locate and commune with a representation of the water element: a stream, a river, a fountain, a canal, a lake, a pond, snow, ice, or the ocean. Enjoy its beauty and notice how it moves and sounds as you think to yourself, "Water, water, water, water…"

Then start once again with the earth element.

Repeat as many times as you'd like or for as long as you have time. After just a short period of time, you will begin to feel the alive presence of nature and the interweaving of the spirit element underneath and within all things.

Thank each element and then go on your way.

## Home Environment Tune-Up

Because you're so sensitive, it's extra important for you to live in a space that nourishes and uplifts you. Here's a holistic practice to help you improve the vibrations in your space. It includes a simple but effective space clearing ritual at the end. (All you need for the ritual is a chime or bell.)

For the full effect, it's best if you can set aside an entire day, or at least a good chunk of a day, for cleaning and clutter clearing. It's best if you don't feel rushed, so you can be as fully present as possible as you clean. Otherwise, just do what you can with the time you have.

Put on any kind of music you're in the mood for. If you're in the mood for angry or harsh music, don't shy away from it. You want to start by getting in touch with your present-moment feelings and mood. Music you're in the mood to hear will help meet you wherever you are and then it can help get your emotions flowing. This means your emotions are likely to change as you clean, so be attuned to that as well. Change the music as you go in order to fit what you're in the mood to hear.

Also light a naturally scented candle or a stick of incense. You can also diffuse essential oil if you prefer. Again, choose according to whatever you're in the mood for. (Be mindful of small children and animals, for whom scents can be overly harsh or even harmful. You can always skip the scent if you're at all concerned.)

Once you've set the mood, begin clearing clutter and cleaning. You don't have to get to everything; just do whatever is calling to you. Maybe today it will just be your closet or your kitchen, or maybe you have a small space and you have time to do an overall clearing and cleaning. The point is to fine-tune your environment in ways that will calm, center, and nourish you, so take your time and take care of yourself in this way. As you do this, you may want to start a list of home improvement actions you can take in the future that will also nourish you, such as painting a room or adding a plant here or there. Approach this process with love and care for yourself and your home. Continue until you've done all you can for the day.

Then pick up the chime (or bell) and open your front door as far as it will go. Strike the chime in the threshold as you set the intention to clear away all obstacles to blessings and to improve the vibration in your space. Each time you ring the chime, imagine peace, harmony, and clarity moving outward with the sound. Once you've rung the chime a few times in the threshold, close the door.

**Strike the chime in the threshold as you set the intention to clear away all obstacles to blessings and to improve the vibration in your space. Each time you ring the chime, imagine peace, harmony, and clarity moving outward with the sound.**

Next, move in a general counterclockwise direction throughout your home, as well as throughout each room and area of your home, ringing or striking the chime as you go. So, for example, you might move in a counterclockwise direction through your foyer, then move to whatever room is adjacent to the foyer when generally moving in a counterclockwise direction through the entire space. Then ring the chime as you move in a counterclockwise direction through that room, etc. The direction and order aren't terribly important, so don't worry about them too much. The important thing is that you ring the chime around the edges of each room and area of your home while setting the intention to clear and harmonize the space. (If there are any animals that will be frightened by the sound, be mindful of them. You can always come back to an area later when your animal friend is no longer in it.)

When you've rung the chime everywhere in your space, return to your front door. Leave it closed, but stand just inside it, facing inward toward your house. Close your eyes, take some deep breaths, and call on the Divine in a way that feels powerful for you. Ask the Divine to fill and surround your space with divine energy and light. You can imagine that light in any color that feels calming and uplifting to you. Set some intentions for how you'd like to feel in your space, and invoke any specific conditions you'd like to call in. Feel gratitude to the Divine and give thanks.

.............

I highly suggest making all three of these rituals a regular part of your spiritual practice. In time, they will become like second nature, and they will help you feel calm, safe, inspired, powerful, and joyfully at home in the world.

**Tess Whitehurst** *believes life is magical. She's the author of lots of books and oracle decks about magical and spiritual living, including the best-selling* Magical Housekeeping, *the award-winning* The Magic of Flowers, *and her latest,* The Self-Love Superpower: The Magical Art of Approving of Yourself (No Matter What). *As the cohost of the* Magic Monday *podcast, she gets to talk to fascinating magical authors and practitioners almost every week. She's also the founder and facilitator of the* Wisdom Circle Online School of Magical Arts. *Tess lives in the* Rocky Mountains *of* Colorado *with her family, which consists of one husband and one cat. Learn more about* Tess *and find her free spells, rituals, and guided meditations at* TessWhitehurst.com.

**Illustrator: Bri Hermanson**

# Psych Yourself Up! Get Balanced, Focused, and Ready for Anything

*Lupa*

It's a full moon in the middle of summer. I'm twenty years old and standing alone in a field surrounded by white oak forests. Four candles—two white, two silver—burn in holders set in the rain-damp grass. I wear my favorite ritual gown, a vintage white dress older than I am, reflecting the moonlight as it sifts through openings in the clouds overhead. Holding my athame in my hand, I call that lunar energy into myself, filling up my heart until it spills over and flushes away the stress, anger, and fear I've felt from years of trauma. Silver light

like water floods my very being, and I feel that for another month I can continue facing the challenges of the days ahead.

We humans are complicated animals, and our ancestors evolved progressively bigger brains as one of their adaptations to an ever-changing world. Not only does our current *Homo sapiens* brain allow us to create, use, and reflect on spiritual and transformative experiences, but it also gives us a deep, sometimes labyrinthine inner landscape to explore and understand. Psychology is one of the tools that we have created to help us better understand ourselves: the universe in contemplation of itself.

In the example above, I used a monthly esbat ritual not only to celebrate my connection to the moon and my patron goddess Artemis, but also to give myself a psychological and spiritual cleansing. Doing this on a regular basis helped me to manage long-term mental health issues and regain resilience to deal with more day-to-day challenges. The colors I chose were deliberate. White and silver are traditionally associated with lunar energy, and they inspired within me feelings of calm, purification, and renewal.

I've also used my work with animal and other nature spirits to help me through tough times. For example, every time I interview for a new job or contract, I ask American Badger and River Otter for help. Badger brings tenacity and groundedness, while Otter reminds me that I should be enjoying what I do every day, even work. Their energy supports my goals, but it also helps me prepare mentally for the challenge of answering questions, promoting my work, and finding out what I need to know about the entity I'm interviewing with. Without that preparation, I might be more nervous and less confident, which makes it less likely that I'll land the job or contract. Even when I've been in dire straits during long periods of unemployment, knowing I can call on these two guides for help has kept me motivated throughout the grueling job hunt.

## So How Does Magic Work?

Opinions vary as to how literally effective magic is. For some Pagans, magic has widespread effects on the external world, while for others it is largely a psychological exercise that happens internally. Regardless of whether you feel there's something more to it or not, there's no denying that there is a lot of psychology involved in magic.

As one example, all of the correspondences, tools, trappings, and symbols are geared to help trip switches in our minds that get us into a better mindset for creating change in accordance with will. Many of them are effective outside of ritual practices, too. Research on how colors can affect our mood, for example, shows that at least in Western societies the color red can make a person feel more powerful and assertive, while blue is calming and peaceful. Many people choose to paint rooms or wear clothing in colors that positively affect their emotions on an everyday basis, and that same strategy can be used to create more effective rituals.

The nice thing about learning the meanings of these various concepts and items is that we can put them to conscious use, not just to create better rituals but also to improve overall mental wellness. And we don't necessarily have to create formal rituals or spells to get an effect, though some people may get better results from more complicated workings. Just by deliberately choosing to wear a certain color or a piece of jewelry that we feel imbues us with a given trait, we can set the tone for our entire day. At the same time, there are reasons that many people go to a lot of trouble choosing the exact items and decorations to use for a given ritual, to help add more meaning and power to the setting in which the magic is to take place.

Carefully chosen ritual elements can help us feel more grounded and effective in a world that is largely out of our control. As an individual person, I can't single-handedly change the big problems that we're facing in this world, whether that's climate change, extreme wealth inequality, social injustice, or other such things. Many of the problems I face, even though they may be more localized or personal, still have their roots in greater systemic imbalances. While I can take actions against the individual tendrils that weave their way through my life, I know that this alone will not create larger change.

**Each ritual or spell that I do empowers me, and I feel like I have more of a handle on the situation. Through these acts, I am able to shake myself out of a downward mental spiral. It's like a big spiritual pep talk.**

But just as cleaning one corner of a messy room helps me feel instantly better, so does addressing one challenge out of many give me the motivation to keep going. These small victories add up, and they give me realistic goals to work toward. Each ritual or spell that I do empowers me, and I feel like I have more of a handle on the situation. Through these acts, I am able to shake myself out of a downward mental spiral that might otherwise lead me to feel defeated. It's like a big spiritual pep talk.

## Bringing Back the Basics: Ground, Center, Shield

There are many ways that you can utilize magical practice to improve your mental health, and I'd like to share a few ideas. I do want to note that nothing in this article is meant to replace formal mental health care, and although I have a master's degree in counseling psychology, I am not your therapist, nor am I offering these ideas and practices as treatment. These are merely some exercises that can help you with overall mental wellness and stress relief.

*Ground, center, shield.* These three practices are at the heart of many magical traditions and are often the first things newcomers learn. There's good reason for that, since the skills they teach are the foundations for more complicated practices. But they can also be used to help with mental wellness, even without a particular magical purpose.

How? It's all about the intent. Many people assume that grounding, centering, and shielding (GCS) need to be done in response to some magical or spiritual disruption, or as part of a formal ritual. Yet you can just as easily use your favorite GCS practices to help you when you're experiencing some sort of psychological distress, whether as part of an ongoing issue or in the form of a sudden upset or trauma.

You can use all three portions of GCS, or whichever one you need the most in the moment. If you're feeling distracted, disconnected, or even dissociated, grounding can help get you rooted back in the present moment and place. Centering is useful when the "brain weasels" get going, those anxious or otherwise out-of-control thoughts that can easily leave you feeling scattered and unbalanced. Shielding is a wonderful practice when you need to feel safe and secure or just want a boost of confidence; it's like a suit of armor that helps you walk more powerfully in the world.

The three examples I'd like to share are just one set of GCS practices that may be used to improve mental wellness or banish stress.

### Countdown to Calm

One of my favorite mindfulness-based grounding exercises is commonly used in counseling practices and can be used literally anywhere and anytime. In the space of a few seconds, you can disrupt negative mental cycles and bring your attention back to the here and now, especially if you've just experienced some sort of mental or emotional upset and need to refocus.

Look around you and identify five things you can see—any five things at all, it doesn't matter which. Next, identify four things you can touch, and then three things you can hear. Find two things you can smell, and then one you could (at least in theory) safely taste. Repeat as necessary until your awareness has returned to the present moment and place, and anytime you feel yourself being carried away by worry or other distractions.

### Centering in Connection

To then center yourself, focus on how the air around you is touching not only you, but everything you just identified, and you are all immersed together in this sea of life-giving oxygen and other elements. Breathe in deeply, and hold for a moment, feeling the air molecules fill your lungs and imagining the oxygen being carried off by your bloodstream to all the cells of your body. At the same time, feel the energy of the place you are in enter your solar plexus with every breath, stabilizing you both within yourself and within this place. Feel that center of energy feeding power to every part of yourself, connecting you to the land wherever you currently are.

### Put on Your Game Face

This practice is a little more elaborate than the others, and draws on physical media as well as your own mind, but it's a good example of where tools and trappings can boost the psychological as well as the magical effectiveness of a ritual.

Let's say you have a difficult conversation ahead of you. Maybe you have to speak with someone with whom there may be a conflict, or you have an interview or talk to give and you're anxious about public speaking. Perhaps you have a legal case to deal with and an approaching court date. Whatever it is, you can use ritual face paint to help you become the best version of you to meet this challenge.

You can use either regular makeup or commercial/costume face paint for this. First, think of times when you have exhibited the qualities you need to bring to bear now. If you're having trouble thinking of them in yourself, bring to mind people, spirits, deities, and even fictional beings who embody those qualities. Next, design makeup or face paint that symbolizes these qualities and/or beings; you can draw it out on a piece of paper first if you'd like.

When the time comes to add this design to your face, create a clean, uncluttered space, then spend a few moments clearing your mind and focusing on the task ahead. As you begin to add makeup or paint to your face, watch as you transform yourself into this ideal self. Feel the power and energy rise within you with each color and design, knowing that even as you draw inspiration from outside of you, there is a corresponding piece of you inside that you are calling forth.

Once the design is complete, spend a few moments looking at yourself in the mirror. Meditate on how you have brought forth this part of yourself in response to your need. Feel the energy of the design and its inspiration soak into you, infusing every cell in your body with its power so that it is an indelible part of you.

If you have used makeup and are able to keep it on throughout your challenge, this will give you an extra boost. Even if you have to remove the makeup or paint, know that the pattern you have created is still there in spirit, and that it symbolizes the best of what you have to offer. Remember it as you go forth into the fray.

**Lupa** *is an author, artist, and naturalist in the Pacific Northwest. She is the author of several books on nature-based Paganism, as well as the creator of the* Tarot of Bones *and* Pocket Osteomancy *divination sets. More information about Lupa and her works may be found at www.thegreenwolf.com.*

**Illustrator: M. Kathryn Thompson**

# Lightning Rod: Magical Techniques for Grounding Anxiety

Dallas Jennifer Cobb

I have lived with anxiety for years, a constriction that causes my guts to spasm, my chest to tighten, and my throat to constrict. I notice my heart racing, my face flushing, profuse sweating, and quick, shallow breathing. I want to share my techniques for preventing and treating anxiety, effectively managing and reducing its negative effects.

## Early Anxiety

In high school I changed schools, and in university I failed a class, because I couldn't overcome the anxiety that kept

me from public speaking. As a young adult, I was terrified at times to leave my house, fearful of crowds and confined spaces, and even anxious about having people sit behind me or not being able to see the exit of whatever room I was in.

Over time I became aware that there were specific situations, energies, and interactions that produced anxiety, so I learned how to avoid them. But anxiety could also hit me like a lightning bolt—sudden, severe, and seemingly out of nowhere. I once burst into tears and fled a social gathering because it was all too much for me.

Instead of just avoiding situations that triggered anxiety, I learned a lot of tricks for calming myself and minimizing and alleviating anxiety. I began to feel more able to navigate life without paralyzing anxiety attacks, and I thought that with my well-honed skills and extensive experience, my days of being paralyzed by anxiety were over.

## The Return of Anxiety

But...during the pandemic, my anxiety returned.

It wasn't just me. I observed increased levels of anxiety in people all around me. They were anxious and overcome with worry. During the early days of the pandemic and lockdown, it seemed that we were all being constantly bombarded with frightening media images of suffering, illness, and death everywhere we turned. The very fabric of our daily lives was changing, literally every day.

There were few known entities that could be relied on for stability and constancy, and even the newness of this way of life felt anxiety-inducing. Encouraged to stay at home, avoid people, wear a mask, and not touch anyone, I was isolated, alone, and frightened.

I wasn't able to visit friends, have a meal with family, see my daughter or companion, or go to social events. Aware of how alone I was, I became more and more anxious. What would happen if I got sick? Would anyone notice? Could I die at home and no one would know?

These fears folded in on me, and I became paranoid of people—all people, everywhere—because during the pandemic we didn't know who was going to make us sick, and potentially anyone we came in contact with could be carrying a deadly disease. It is no wonder xenophobia, aggression, and racism were on the rise. We were primed to be on guard against an invisible attacker.

## Relieving Anxiety

To relieve my anxiety, I looked to a variety of techniques: medical, psycho-educational, scientific, and spiritual or magical ones.

The medical techniques I had learned years earlier were the basis of my strategy. I remembered the simple practice of biofeedback, and began to use long, conscious breathing to slow down my elevated heart rate and deepen my shallow breathing. Research taught me about the vagus nerve, and how a longer exhalation activates it and sends the body messages of safety, calming the autonomic nervous system.

I learned that anxiety is an activation of the sympathetic nervous system, leading to a state of hyperarousal as a result of perceiving danger. The nervous system moves into survival mode and responds with a fight, flight, or freeze reaction. My historical pattern was flight. I would run away from whatever frightened me, but at times I would also freeze. This reaction served a purpose: it was designed to keep me safe.

## What Lightning Looks Like

Not wanting to shut down the messages of unsafety from my nervous system, I chose instead to pay attention to them. I began to catalog them, making a list of "what triggers me." Every time I found myself experiencing anxiety, I tried to identify what had triggered it. Sometimes that process took a long time, especially when I was so deeply triggered that it took days for me to come out of anxiety. By writing the triggers down, I created a long list in my notebook, and became consciously aware of those triggers. I was able to see what stimulated the lightning bolt of anxiety.

Awareness of the triggers made it far easier for me to begin avoiding them. I knew what lightning looked like, and I could avoid it before it struck me. I turned off the news, avoided TV, stopped reading comments on social media, and even avoided nervous conversations with neighbors about the unknowns associated with the pandemic. Avoidance is a great preventive measure to minimize anxiety.

## Grounding Anxiety

Not all anxiety can simply be avoided, because life is full of surprises and unknown factors. To counteract the feeling of anxiety striking me like lightning, I started another list entitled "reset buttons." This was a list of all the practices, substances, people, places, and things that helped me reset my nervous system. The list included my allies, who were people I knew loved and cared for me. Contact with them blessed me with a sense of safety, and I was able to calm myself.

My list of reset buttons also included taking a bath or shower and feeling the renewal of energy through water immersion; sleeping; eating a protein-rich meal so my body was nourished and supported; walking, running, and exercising; spending time with my animals; and quietly reading a book. I learned that many of these practices involve a limbic bond with another being (human or animal), a connection that helps to regulate the nervous system.

Spending time in nature, hiking, camping, and exploring became some of my regular weekly activities. Contact with the earth made me feel better. I learned about the practice of grounding: placing my bare feet in contact with the earth in order to become attuned to its electromagnetic energy. Research shows that this interaction can produce physiological change in humans, activating the parasympathetic nervous system to decrease anxiety (Ober, Sinatra, and Zucker 2010). The more items that went on my list of reset buttons, the more empowered I felt to deal with anxiety when it arose.

## Magic and Science

While new neuroscience research has deeply informed my understanding of anxiety, I have also found spiritual practices that enable me to change my consciousness at will, which is how Dion Fortune defined magic. I learned how to change my internal landscape from lead to gold, from anxiety to empowered awareness. These techniques are like a lightning rod that grounds the energy from the bolts of anxiety that in the past had shot me into a hyper-aroused state. Several of these practices work quickly and powerfully and provide noticeable relief. They can be used preventively, before anxiety strikes, or as a treatment if it does. These techniques are transformative magical and practical tools to ground anxiety.

## Incantation

An incantation is commonly defined as a series of words said as a magic spell or charm. While trying to find ways to transform my anxiety, I came across a technique called "notice and name." Just like it sounds, it is the simple process of using words as a magic spell to notice the effects of anxiety and name them.

Because word sounds have power, and the use of the voice can break the spell of being frozen in fear, noticing and naming can help to ground the charge of anxiety. Simply stating what is going on takes the power away from the effect and makes it something I now have some control over. For example:

*My belly is clenched and my heart is racing. I feel filled with fear.*

Just saying something like that out loud enables me to be consciously aware, in the moment, of what is going on, and to recognize the root of it: fear.

Once I have practiced noticing and naming, and now know what lies behind the sensations in my body, I can more easily take action to seek a sense of safety. That noticing and naming brings me into the present and makes me part of the process, so now it is not something that just happens to me but is something I experience. That small shift really does transform the experience in the moment, and empowers me.

## Herbal Helpers

There are many herbs available that have a calming effect on the nervous system. I avoid stimulants like caffeine, because of the long-term negative effects, and I also avoid herbs with suppressant or depressant qualities to them, such as valerian, CBD, and cannabis. I seek out herbs with calming, soothing qualities and prefer those that are easy to obtain, affordable, and effective. My favorites are chamomile, lemon balm and lavender. They work wonders on the nervous system.

### Chamomile

Chamomile (*Matricaria chamomilla*) is native to North America, commonly grows wild, and has a pleasant smell and taste. Best used in a tea, chamomile has a mild flavor and combines well with other herbs. It calms and soothes the nervous system.

### Lemon Balm

Lemon balm (*Melissa officinalis*) has a calming effect and is known to relieve anxiety, stress, insomnia, and even dementia. Make a tea of this lemony-mint-tasting herb, and as you sip it, feel the effects of your blood pressure lowering and stress melting away.

### Lavender

Lavender (*Lavandula angustifolia*) is another fragrant flower that has significant healing properties. It is commonly used to treat anxiety, insomnia, depression, and restlessness. I have used lavender to make tea and lavender butter and baked it in shortbread. The essential oil of lavender can be safely diffused in your home and has antiseptic and anti-inflammatory properties.

## Crystals to Ground and Calm

There are many crystals that have a grounding and calming effect on the nervous system. I keep them in my pocket or bra and place them next to the bath and on my bedside table. Three of the most common and readily available options are amethyst, rose quartz, and black tourmaline.

### Amethyst

Amethyst is purple and is said to promote clarity and relaxation by absorbing stress and "negative" energy. I keep amethyst next to my bed because of its role in absorbing anxiety, which can cause insomnia.

### Rose Quartz

Rose quartz is soft pink and is linked to self-compassion and emotional healing. I keep rose quartz in the bathroom because it reminds me to gently care for myself and to hold myself in love, peace, and ease.

### Black Tourmaline

Black tourmaline is something I keep tucked in my bra or pocket. It absorbs negativity and can work wonders against toxic energy or attack. It promotes calm, stability, and a sense of safety.

## Permanent Lightning Rods

Whether or not we have future waves of pandemic conditions, social isolation, and/or lockdowns, I now know that I have myriad tools to help me feel safer in unusual and unpredictable situations.

I know my triggers and can, to some degree, avoid them. I know what resets my nervous system after being triggered, and I can employ these practices after I have encountered something that I can neither control nor avoid.

Going forward, I know that when I experience anxiety, I don't have to flee a situation or change schools, and I don't have to project my unnamed fears onto others. Instead of acting out in xenophobic, racist, agoraphobic, or socially anxious ways, I can draw on my medical, scientific, and magical tools to help ground the lightning of anxiety.

## Resources

Ober, Clinton, Stephen Sinatra, and Martin Zucker. *Earthing: The Most Important Health Discovery Ever?* Laguna Beach, CA: Basic Health Publications. 2010.

Porges, Stephen W. "Neuroception: A Subconscious System for Detecting Threats and Safety." *Zero to Three* 24, no. 5 (May 2004): 19–24. https://chhs.fresnostate.edu/ccci/documents/07.15.16%20Neuroception%20Porges%202004.pdf. Accessed March 3, 2022.

**Dallas Jennifer Cobb** *lives in a magical village on Lake Ontario. A Pagan, mother, feminist, writer, and animal lover, she enjoys a sustainable lifestyle with a balance of time and money. Widely published, she writes about what she knows: brain injury, magick, herbs, astrology, healing, recovery, and vibrant sustainability. When she isn't communing with nature, she likes to correspond with like-minded beings. Reach her at jennifer.cobb@live.com.*

**Illustrator: M. Kathryn Thompson**

# Confident Witchcraft

*Melanie Marquis*

To succeed in magick requires genuine confidence, yet there is not a witch on earth who hasn't felt that dull ache of doubt or twitch of hesitancy in their heart exactly at the moment that they most need to manifest unwavering belief and courage. Perhaps you are new to the Craft and you're not sure about the spell you're doing. Maybe you're uncertain about the approach you're taking to the magick, or even wondering whether the overall goal and intention is in fact the best path to pursue. You might just be in an emotional slump and feeling down on yourself or anxious.

When confidence slips, it's essential to get it back if you want to be as effective and successful as possible, both in magick and in life in general. Only with confidence can doubts and obstacles be cleared away to make room for magick to flourish. Not all your spells are going to work 100 percent as intended. But if you don't believe in your magick, it doesn't stand a chance of working. Fortunately, there are lots of ways to build and strengthen your confidence as a witch so that you'll have a deeper well to draw from whenever you need it.

## Believe in More Than Yourself

When I'm feeling less confident than I'd like, I have to resist the tendency to just avoid doing magick altogether. I know the magick can succeed only if I'm able to push past all those doubtful feelings and be absolutely positive about what I'm doing, which takes both mental and emotional effort that I don't always feel like I can muster. It's easier to just avoid it completely and do nothing when I feel like whatever I attempt to do is bound to fail. That whole thought trap, however, is based on the false premise that I am only as big as my personality and my feelings. The truth is I am much larger than that, as I am much more than that. I am a part of all that is, and as a witch, I can tap into this limitless power to which I am intrinsically connected. To be confident in my witchcraft requires me to be confident in only two simple facts: there is much more to the universe than only me, and magick goes far beyond only me. Confidence is a state of mind, and you can put your mind there at any time by remembering who and what you truly are: an essential part of all that is.

Witchcraft involves tapping into something that goes far beyond the individual. A witch is a conduit for power, but not the sole source of it. We are keepers of the power, keepers of the cauldron, watchers of the well—but we did not create this power, nor can we manifest it out of nothing. Your power as a witch comes down to how well you are able to open yourself up and let powers much larger than you flow through you, and how well you are able to confidently command those forces. While both components can be enhanced and developed through study and practice, we are all unique and we each have our own strengths and weaknesses. Some of the skills used in magick might come to you very easily, while others require more effort and practice. A new witch might excel in entering a trance state, for instance, finding it an easy and natural thing to do, while a more experienced witch might have to devote more time and technique to it. While experience is invaluable and there's truly no substitute for it, it also isn't the be-all and end-all of magick.

## Be Genuine

We've all heard the advice "fake it till you make it," but when it comes to witchcraft, faking it will only get you so far. Faking it can help kick-start confidence and is useful for shaking off minor stresses and doubts, but real, lasting confidence must be built upon a foundation of truth, belief, and ability. Being honest and genuine in your practice is a big part of building your skills and deepening your craft as a witch. That means being truthful with yourself about what you can and can't do, and honoring what makes sense to you as an independently thinking and feeling human being. If you don't understand why you're doing each part of a spell, it's difficult to have confidence in what you're doing. Stick with magick that makes sense to you, even if it seems overly simple. It's better to choose a straightforward spell with an operation and elements that you fully understand than to half-heartedly fumble through something overly elaborate or complex that seems to go against your own powers of logic and intuition. If you know why you're doing something, you will feel much more confident in doing it, and the magick is much more likely to succeed as expected.

## Learning the Building Blocks of Magick

Confidence requires ability. Without the power and skills to back it up, confidence in one's witchcraft can quickly fade. This doesn't mean that you have to learn everything there is to know or precisely follow a strict and complex structure before you can successfully make magick. While your practices do need to have a strong foundation and a solid, logical framework in order to succeed, you can build pretty much whatever you like upon that basic blueprint.

Knowledge is power, and the more you know, the better equipped you are to improvise and be creative. While every witch has their favorite tools and techniques of magick, it's good to have a broad base of knowledge to draw on in your practice. Witch studies vary widely, as witches vary widely. There is no standard set of information that must be learned, and it's up to you to discover what might be useful to you in your own practice. Whether it's learning about the properties of stones and minerals, studying astronomy and astrology, studying ancient symbols, learning to compound herbs into potions and powders, or something else entirely, explore what calls to you, and strive to learn and practice as much as you can. As your knowledge and experience grow, so too will your confidence.

**Knowledge is power, and the more you know, the better equipped you are to improvise and be creative. While every witch has their favorite tools and techniques of magick, it's good to have a broad base of knowledge to draw on in your practice.**

## Magick in the Public Eye

Witchcraft has grown and changed dramatically over the past two decades. Many witches today were born into a world of internet, smartphones, and social media, making it easier than ever to find other witches and share ideas. While that part of this progression is wonderful, it also makes it easier than ever to open ourselves to the opinions and judgments of others, which can either help or hinder a witch's confidence. Today, a growing number of witches choose to post their spells, altar photos, and magickal advice and questions online, for all to scrutinize. While it can be nice to have a network available for new ideas and feedback, exposing one's magick to the Wi-Fi world at large definitely invites criticism, which in turn can hurt your confidence.

In the past, most witches did their magick hidden deep in the wilderness or behind closed doors. The only feedback on their magick came from the universe itself: either a spell worked or it didn't. Remember that your magick is between yourself and whatever powers of the universe you choose to work with. It doesn't matter how many "likes" your altar photos or candle spells get. What matters is whether or not the magick worked as intended, and whether or not you learned something in the process. If you choose to share your magickal practices with the world, don't ever let the opinions of other people weigh you down or hurt your confidence. You can see firsthand whether or not your spells are working. Let the magick speak for itself.

## Talismans to Boost Confidence

Let's face facts: while Dumbo didn't exactly *need* the feather, it certainly didn't hurt, either! It's nice to feel as though we are getting a little help along our journey, even when we know that the biggest changes must come from within. For a ready-made talisman to boost your confidence, try carrying a tiger's-eye, a quartz crystal, or a piece of jade. Herbs to increase confidence include cinnamon, ginger, and orange. Try sprinkling the herbs on the Emperor or the Sun tarot card, wrapping it in a white cloth and carrying it with you to help give your confidence levels a boost. Carrying an acorn, or wearing a symbol of the sun or moon, can also magnify your feelings of confidence. You can also try wearing metals, stones, scents, and colors that are considered lucky for your zodiac sign. Doing so will help raise your vibration and fortify your power.

## Respect Your Own Authority

Every witch must come to realize and believe in their own authority and ability to make magick. It is an integral part of what is meant by standing in your own power as a witch. Witchcraft never did, and never does, ask for permission. You don't have to practice for ages before you can be confident in your witchcraft. In fact, you already have everything within you that's required to effectively make magick. Let go of the false limitations that you and others might be placing on your craft, and delve into the aspects of magick that call to you. All you need is a little self-exploration and observation to help you gain confidence and unlock your limitless potential.

**Melanie Marquis** *is the creator of the* Modern Spellcaster's Tarot *(illustrated by Scott Murphy) and the author of several books, including* A Witch's World of Magick; The Witch's Bag of Tricks; Carl Llewellyn Weschcke: Pioneer and Publisher of Body, Mind & Spirit; Witchy Mama *(with Emily A. Francis)*; Beltane; Lughnasadh; *and* Llewellyn's Little Book of Moon Spells. *The founder of* United Witches *global coven, producer of* Mystical Minds Convention, *and a local coordinator for the* Pagan Pride Project, *Melanie loves sharing magick with others and has presented workshops and rituals to audiences across the* US. *She lives in* Denver, CO.

**Illustrator: Tim Foley**

# Witchy Living

## Day-by-Day Witchcraft

# Making Mundane Moments Magickal: Find the Mystery in Everything You Do

*Phoenix LeFae*

Have you ever woken up, logged on to your social media, and realized, with horror and disappointment, that the previous night was the full moon? Yep, you missed it...again. This is a familiar feeling for me. There have been times when I've felt like a bad witch, and not in the fun way, because I missed an important astrological moment, or haven't worked a spell in months, or haven't been to a ritual for even longer.

I call this feeling the B.S. Bad Witch Blues, or BSBWB, which is the social expectation that witchcraft needs to look a certain way or only comes in the form of ritual, meditation, and spells. Well, I'm here to relieve you of any BSBWB. Because guess what? Being a magickal practitioner doesn't mean you have to conform to specific full moon practices, sabbat rituals, or anything else. Magick can be in the form of whatever works for you.

A magickal life, a witch's life, is one where magick and mystery are woven through all the moments of our lives. This includes everything—yes, everything—from brushing your teeth to driving your car to cleaning the kitchen. This might sound impossible, but I promise it's true: even the most mundane moments contain all the magick you could possibly desire.

**A magickal life, a witch's life, is one where magick and mystery are woven through all the moments of our lives. This includes everything—yes, everything—from brushing your teeth to driving your car to cleaning the kitchen.**

The difference between a mundane moment and a magickal moment is your personal approach. Yes, this is one of those examples where your intention really is everything. What we consider to be mundane activities might feel like a drag. These things tend to be more tedious, boring, or difficult. At first glance it might not look like there is anything inherently magickal about them. The less we *like* the activity, the further removed it might seem from magick. But the truth is the world is magick. We are magick. And therefore, everything we do and interact with is also magickal.

## Ritualizing Life

When we are able to simply shift our perspective, we can make anything we have to do magickal. There will always be tasks that must be done, whether we like it or not, so why not allow magick to flow through those activities? Here are some ways to make any mundane moment magickal.

### The Magick of Cleaning

Cleaning is a part of life. Dishes need to be washed, laundry must be done, toilets need to be scrubbed. Rather than slog through these moments annoyed and frustrated, focus your magickal intention for the work at hand. Here are some ways to start:

- When washing dishes, focus on your breathing and the connection to water. Allow the dishwashing process to become a meditation.
- Toilets hold a lot of negative energy. When you scrub the toilet, use it as a time to clear out that negative energy. Draw sigils or symbols of protection in the bowl with the scrubber.
- When you put a load of laundry into the washing machine, add a pinch of blessed salt or herbs for success in with the soap. This will wash your clothes in blessings and successful energy.
- Before you vacuum, sprinkle vacuum powders that have been magickally charged across your floors. This offers a spiritual cleanse on top of your regular cleaning. As you vacuum, all the negative energy will be sucked up into the machine. Make sure you change or clean the vacuum bag when done.
- Washing windows is the perfect time to recharge your wards.
- Sweep your home from back to front and out the front door. This will clear away negative energy and banish it from your home.

## The Magick of Food

We all eat. For some of us, cooking, food, and being in the kitchen may already feel like magick. But for others, cooking, food, and being in the kitchen may feel like a lot of work and no fun at all. Cooking with intention is important. The energy you hold while you are cooking makes its way into the food you prepare. You and your family eat that energy.

We might look at cooking and eating as mundane activities, but at the very core of them is the power of life force. Eating keeps our bodies functioning. Eating literally keeps us alive. And no matter what we choose to eat, we are taking in the life force of another thing. What's not magickal about that? Here are some ways to add a dash of ritual and magick to cooking and eating as a way to reinforce your connection to the mysterious:

- Say a prayer of gratitude over your food before eating. Take a moment to hold gratitude for the plants, animals, farmers, truck drivers, and cooks that made it possible for you to eat this food.
- Speak out loud prayers of health, wealth, and gratitude over any food you cook.
- Draw sigils or magickal symbols over your plate of food before consuming your meal. This will infuse the food with the power of that sigil. As you eat, hold awareness of that magickal act.
- Use herbs, spices, or other ingredients that are in magickal alignment with any spell goals that you are working on to the foods that you prepare.
- Add herbs, spices, or other ingredients that are in magickal alignment to any spell goals that you are working on to water bottles, and drink in those magickal intentions throughout the day.
- Draw sigils or magickal symbols on your water bottle or coffee cup to help imbue everything you drink with magickal energy.

- Burn bay leaves or onion peels in your kitchen to clear out negative energy.
- Cut a lemon in half, place it on a plate, and put it in the center of any room where you want to clear out negative energy. Once the lemon begins to turn, toss it out.

### The Magick of Bathing

Bathing is another regular part of life. There is something very sensual about bathing. Instead of just focusing on scrubbing our armpits, we can allow ourselves to take some time to connect with all our senses. Ritual baths where we add herbs and oils, light candles, play music, and luxuriate all day are lovely, but I don't always have that kind of time. You don't have to spend hours in the tub to make bathing a magickal moment. Here are some ideas:

- Make a salt scrub with your favorite essential oils. Use this at the end of your regular shower to connect to magick.
- Feel the water. That might seem like an obvious thing, but *really* feel the water. Connect with the energy of the water as it touches your body.
- After you've completed your washing, take a moment to "wash" your spirit. Scan your body to see where there may be stuck energy or things that need to be released. Let the water do its job and clear that out—watch it flow down the drain.
- Use magickally charged soaps. There are a lot of cool, inexpensive magickal soaps out there! Or better yet, learn to make your own.
- Create an altar or shrine in your bathroom. This could be for health and wellbeing, a water spirit, a house spirit, or something else completely. Light candles and/or incense when you bathe as an offering or devotional to that energy.

## Setting Yourself Up for Success with Touchstones

A little prep work is often all we need to change a behavior. Making mundane moments more magickal can be as simple as building a new habit. I love a good, long ritual with singing, dancing, drumming, and lighting changes. I love the drama and craft of ritual. But a good ritual or magickal moment doesn't have to have to be dramatic to be effective. It can be a simple moment. And often our modern lives are too busy for these moments to happen organically, so we can use technology to help us connect with that power.

### Touchstones and Paying Attention

A touchstone is a mundane cue you create to help develop a new habit. Touchstones work like little hints out in the world to help you stay connected to magick. They can be virtually anything. You might pause and offer a blessing when you see the color blue. You might speak a mantra when you make a left turn. Maybe you stop and take three deep intentional breaths any time you wash your hands.

**A touchstone is a mundane cue you create to help develop a new habit. . . . They can be virtually anything. You might pause and offer a blessing when you see the color blue.**

One of my touchstones is to take a deep, grounding breath anytime I put a key in a lock. I use it as an opportunity to ground and redirect my energy. It is a small thing, but deeply magickal and an important part of my daily practice.

One thing to keep in mind with touchstones is that creating the practice can take time. It might take a few days or weeks to build up the practice, like putting a key in a lock. It took me a couple of weeks to develop this practice as part of my muscle memory. When creating a touchstone, don't get discouraged if it doesn't take hold right away. Keep going with it and you'll find that soon it becomes a regular magickal part of your day.

One of the easiest ways of bringing more magick into your mundane life is by connecting with where you live. Make a commitment to take a walk around your block every day. If that's not a physical possibility for you, sit in a window every day. By doing this, you have the opportunity to see the cycles, shifts, and changes that are happening where you live. It allows you to connect with the natural cycles of your living space.

The simple act of paying attention to the world around you will bring a ton of beauty, awe, and magick into what might appear totally mundane. Trust me, it's totally worth it. Here are some other ways to pay attention to the magick that is in your daily life already:

- Set an alarm on your phone to go off at least twice a day with a reminder to breathe or offer gratitude for your life.
- Make walking through a threshold a moment to allow mystery to unfold. The more you pay attention to thresholds, the more mystery you will see in the world around you.
- Use a perfume or essential oil to call in the energy of a deity.
- Notice when your favorite number shows up in the world and make a wish!
- Find a penny? Pick it up! This is a great way to call in more abundance and show gratitude for the gifts that are literally right in front of you.
- Charge a pressure point on your body. We have pressure points all over our bodies that we can connect with a specific magickal feeling, need, or goal. When you press on that pressure point, it will connect you with the magick you are seeking.

- Create a ledger or journal to write down the seasonal changes that you notice. Pay attention to shifts in weather patterns and plant patterns. Make notes on the full and new moons. Look back over your notes to spot patterns and cycles.
- Make a dedicated magickal spot in your home, garden, yard, or neighborhood and commit to spending time there every day. You don't have to bring offerings, meditate, or do anything else that is specifically "spiritual." Just *be* in that place every day. Allow yourself some time to simply notice what is going on.

The ritual of living is the most magickal part of life. One could argue that life is filled with mundane moments, but I would counter that life is actually full of magickal moments! Big, dramatic rituals with candles and incense are lovely, but connecting with the magick that is happening in our day-to-day lives is the most profound. Life is a mystery. We need only remember that in order to feel it. The more we remember, the more we feel—and the magick grows exponentially.

**Phoenix LeFae** *(she/her) is equal parts blue-eyed wanderer and passionate devotee to several deities. Her journey with witchcraft started in 1993, when her athame was a wooden-handled butter knife stolen from her mom's kitchen. Her love of magick and mystery has led her down many paths, lineages, and traditions. She is an initiate in the* Reclaiming Tradition *of* Witchcraft, *the* Avalon Druid Order, *and* Gardnerian Wicca. *She has had the pleasure of teaching and leading ritual across the* United States, Canada, *and* Australia. *Phoenix has written several books, including* What Is Remembered Lives, Walking in Beauty, Life Ritualized, *and* Witches, Heretics, and Warrior Women. *She is a professional witch and the owner of the esoteric* Goddess *shop* Milk & Honey, *www.Milk-and-Honey.com.*

**Illustrator: Bri Hermanson**

# Renewing Your Magickal Self Through Cleaning Up and Letting Go

*Ari & Jason Mankey*

Cleaning out a closet or a set of dresser drawers is not an activity most people look forward to. Going for a walk in the woods is far more pleasant, but tidying up and getting rid of unused items can be a magickal exercise. Magick is more than candle spells and herbal potions. Anything that involves the clearing out of unwanted energy has the potential to be magickal!

Organize
ARCHIVE

## Cleaning Out Our Mundane Spaces

Clothes are more than items we wear so that we are allowed into restaurants; they are also a reflection of who we are as people and often commemorate certain experiences. Picking up a band T-shirt at a concert is an example of a piece of clothing that is a keepsake and a snapshot of who we are and our personal preferences. Wearing a shirt with a graphic featuring a superhero or a favorite cartoon character is a way to share something we love with everyone we meet and to indulge our inner child. Clothes without labels have their own power, too. A warm, fuzzy sweater can instantly bring back the memory of a perfect autumn day.

Clothes have the power to stir up a variety of emotions, but those feelings are not always positive. A certain shirt might remind you of an ex-boyfriend, or maybe a now-former friend gave you a pair of cat socks for your birthday and they now remind you of the bitter feelings you have toward that person. It might feel strange to think of a pair of socks as a trigger, but it happens! This is where the magick of cleaning out a closet comes in handy.

Magick is often about getting rid of energies and powers that no longer serve us. Clearing and cleaning out our clothes is a practical example of this. Opening a drawer and taking a solid look at everything in there might not feel magickal on the outside, but it most certainly is! With a little thought, cleaning out your closet can lead to a transformed you.

When cleaning out anything in your home, the first thing to consider is relevancy. When you look at a shirt or any other object, your first thought should be, "Does this item have a purpose in my life?" In other words, is it relevant? A dress you haven't worn in three years that you don't feel warm and fuzzy about has become irrelevant, and it's time to move on. It's natural to think, "Maybe I'll wear this again," but be honest with yourself about whether that's actually true.

Sometimes things can be relevant, but only because they bring up negative emotions. If there's something lurking in your dresser that brings you pain or anger, cast it out! If there's nothing positive to be gained by keeping an item, why have it around?

Who we are as people will change over the years, and the stuff we collect will often reflect that growth or remind us of who we used to be. None of us are exactly the same person we were ten years ago, and that's because we are constantly experiencing new things. There might have been a time when you wore a lot of black, but now you prefer brighter colors. It's healthy to let go of certain parts of ourselves, and that includes the things that other version of us used to wear.

We often attach a lot of sentimental and emotional energy to inanimate objects, and we should respect the energy we give such items. There's no reason to get rid of a shirt from your deceased grandmother if it reminds you of her. Sadness is mostly seen as a negative emotion, but grief can remind us of the people we love and help us to connect to their energies and memory. Just because you are never going to wear a shirt again doesn't mean you *have* to get rid of it. Something can retain relevancy in our lives even if we don't use it regularly. If the idea of discarding something makes you sad, you should probably keep that item!

It's not necessary to go all Marie Kondo over everything you are getting rid of and wish each item a personal goodbye, but after sorting out a drawer, it can be helpful to say a few words. After we've created a discard pile, we like to take a deep breath and say:

> *I move on this day from what no longer serves me. I embrace the journey ahead while thinking fondly of the positive I've left behind. May the road ahead be filled with magick, mystery, and wonder. So mote it be!*

Cleaning out a closet is about more than tidying up your home or removing things that no longer serve you; it's also about making space for new experiences. Letting go of things from the past frees up space so we can fully grasp the present. Attachments to material things can also keep us stuck in a past that we've mostly outgrown. It's hard to build forward momentum when we are stuck in the past.

When we clean out a drawer or a closet, the energy that's released from that task tells the universe we are ready for new adventures and opportunities. This energy frequently inspires us to seek out fresh experiences on our own, although we often find that the adventures simply come to us after some tidying up. Magick is about putting your intentions out into the universe, and cleaning, clearing, and releasing things will do just that!

**When we clean out a drawer or a closet, the energy that's released from that task tells the universe we are ready for new adventures and opportunities. This energy frequently inspires us to seek out fresh experiences on our own.**

A purge of the wardrobe offers additional magickal opportunities. What we wear is a good example of glamour magick. Sometimes we just feel better about ourselves when wearing a flattering dress or a bad-ass pair of jeans. That feeling manifests as magickal energy and can be felt by those we come into contact with.

Dress-up isn't just a game we play as children; it's something we do as adults, often without thinking about it. We wear different outfits for work, leisure, and sometimes Witch-work. Cultivating a new style every few years can lead to a very different you. We are not what we wear, but what we wear can tap into certain emotions and play into the expectations others have for us. We know that it's not necessary to wear a lot of magickal bling when performing ritual, but necklaces, robes, and bracelets make us feel more magickal, and those feelings are transferred directly into our spellcraft.

**A little bit of order and organization can make decision-making easier and bring about feelings of accomplishment and self-esteem. All of these feelings will also make your spellwork stronger.**

Cleaning and clearing mundane spaces can also bring a sense of order to our lives. Order doesn't mean everything has to be perfectly neat and tidy; it simply means that no matter how you have things arranged, you can find what you are looking for easily. A little bit of order and organization can make decision-making easier and bring about feelings of accomplishment and self-esteem. All of these feelings will also make your spellwork stronger.

## Cleaning Our Magickal Spaces

The spare bedroom in our house is devoted almost entirely to our Witchcraft practice (except when we have a guest staying over). It's full of Books of Shadows, stones and crystals, several dozen bottles of oil, numerous deity statues and magickal tools, and over a dozen candles in various stages of use. In addition, the members of our coven often leave items in our Craft room. It's a small space, yet it's packed to the gills with magickal bric-a-brac and often gets a bit unwieldy.

The accumulation of stuff in our ritual room means that it needs to be cleaned out at least once a year, and it's always a daunting task. There will always be bits of unwanted candle wax haunting our ritual space, but an organized area makes our practice so much easier! We all have different organizational styles, and you'll have to experiment to find the one that works best for you. We just want to share why organizing your magickal space will make your Witchcraft practice stronger.

Since spellwork often involves throwing as much focused energy at a problem as possible, having an organized magickal cupboard makes it easier to put your spells together. If you can easily see all of your oils and herbs, it's that much easier to pick out just the right item to assist you in your spellwork. Keeping all of your crystals on ten random altars in no particular order makes it easy to overlook or forget the crystal that might be just perfect for your working. After running into this problem far too often, we put our most-used stones and crystals on a moon-shaped shelf right at eye level to make finding them much easier.

Crafting a spell can often be about flow. For Witches who rely on their intuition when doing spellwork, assembling the tools for a spell is often done in a trancelike state. In our ritual space, it always feels like Ari is being guided by a higher power when she's putting together a spell, and when she doesn't have to stop and think about where that perfect piece of citrine is hiding, it's easier for her to stay focused on the spell she's casting.

Mundane thoughts interrupt the energies radiating from us that help ensure successful spellcraft. If your thoughts are focused on finding your Road Opener oil ("It's on this shelf, right? How about this one?") and not on your spell, the results will most likely be less than optimal. A bit of organization will help to keep your spellwork on track and reduce distractions.

In our ritual space, we have a place set aside for our Mighty Dead to gather with us, and our entire house is filled with altars to various deities and ancestors. Keeping these places clean and organized makes working with those powers that much easier. It also keeps us in their good graces. Why should my grandparents bother to stick around if I'm just going to let their pictures get dirty? That certainly doesn't feel respectful. Cleaning out the spaces we set aside for deities is also important. Dusting off the Dionysus altar does more than keep Dionysus happy; it draws us closer to him. Touching the objects we've dedicated to him strengthens the bonds between us and the god of the vine.

## The Magickal Self

In magickal practice we often attempt to impose our will on outside forces. Examples of this include "I will have a job I like" and "I will experience love," both pretty common spell ideas. But taming a disorganized ritual room or cleaning out a neglected closet are also examples of imposing our will on an outside force. It may feel like a different kind of magick, but it's still magick. We use magick to take control of our lives and to create the type of world we wish to live in.

Most importantly, there's no separation between our magickal self and our mundane self. There are certainly times when we all feel less magickal than we might like, but even in such moments magick is still all around us and remains a part of us. As Witches, we attempt to continually craft our best magickal life, and sometimes that life involves things that most people think of as mundane or ordinary. But there's still magick in those moments, as well as opportunities for personal growth and transformation. The beauty of Witchcraft is that it can turn something as tedious as tidying up into a magickal act.

**Ari Mankey** *has been practicing Witchcraft and creating spells for over twenty years. Away from the Craft, she has devoted her life to medical laboratory science and developing the perfect whisky ice cream.*

**Jason Mankey** *has written eight books for Llewellyn and is a frequent speaker and teacher at Pagan festivals across North America. He lives in Northern California with his wife, Ari, where they run two local covens. You can follow him on Instagram and Twitter @panmankey.*

**Illustrator: M. Kathryn Thompson**

# Fifty Shades of Magick: Ignite Passion in Love, Lust & Life

*Monica Crosson*

What color do you think of when it comes to love magick? Is it the pink bloom of sweet romance and making love in a room full of roses? How about the crimson red of a heated night of passion in black leather and lace bindings? Or maybe you think of the citrusy glow of a day of self-care, complete with candles and a ritual bath. Whether you're looking to appreciate your own self-worth, stir up romance, rekindle the embers of a dying love, or just enjoy a hot one-night stand, I have fifty shades of magick just for you.

## Love

Are you in the mood for love? Try these tips, spells, and recipes to open your heart and allow love to be your guide.

### 1. Banish Body Insecurity

On a piece of paper, draw a rough image of how you see yourself. Mark an X on all of the areas that you dislike about your physical appearance. Into a lit cauldron, fireproof pot, firepit, etc., toss the illustration. As it burns, repeat: "I am worthy. I appreciate and love my body. I am beautiful."

### 2. Bedroom Blessing

Clean your bedroom and put fresh sheets on the bed. Use cedar and rose incense in a censer or fireproof dish as you walk deosil (clockwise) around the room. As you do this, repeat, "Love resides here." Light candles and sprinkle rose petals across your bedding. Say, "May this room be a setting for peace, love, rest, and respite. Blessed be."

### 3. Love Potion #9

Wear this potion to stimulate desire and increase sexual allure. To 9 ounces carrier oil, add 9 drops each of these essential oils: rose, basil, clove, vanilla, cinnamon, ginger, chamomile, lavender, and bergamot.

### 4. To Stir Up Romance

These foods are the perfect additions to recipes for a night of romance.

*Coriander:* To draw new love

*Chocolate:* Love, attraction

*Cinnamon:* Fertility, arousal

*Vanilla:* Love, romance

*Banana:* Sexual stamina

### 5. A Chocolate Hug

This hot chocolate recipe is guaranteed to stir up some magick. Heat the first six ingredients over medium heat. Whisk in the liqueur, then divide between two mugs and top with whipped cream.

- ⅔ cup dark chocolate chips
- 4 teaspoons cocoa powder
- 1½ cups whole milk
- ½ cup half and half
- ½ teaspoon cinnamon
- Cayenne to taste
- 3–4 tablespoons coffee liqueur
- Whipped cream

### 6. To Keep Love Sweet

Write your name and the name of your lover on a piece of paper and tuck in a small glass jar along with some rose petals. Pour honey to top, secure the lid, and safely burn a pink tea light candle on top of the secured jar. After the flame has safely burned out, place the jar under your bed.

### 7. The Ties That Bind

Knot magick through sensual play can have powerful effects. Focus your intention as each knot is tied. As the sexual energy builds, refocus your combined energies on your intended results.

### 8. To Summon a Lover

On the new moon, take two small red pillar candles (one representing you and the other a new lover) and anoint them with Come to Me Oil (recipe next). Wrap the candles, with three turns each, at the ends of a 24-inch length of ribbon. Wrap three turns every night until the candles come together. Let set until the full moon. Light them both in an outdoor firepit or fireproof container. (They're going to get hot.) As you do this, envision a new lover coming into your life.

### 9. Come to Me Oil

Use this oil in magick to draw love to you. Add 20 drops patchouli, 10 drops rose, and 10 drops jasmine to 8 ounces carrier oil.

### 10. Open Yourself to Love

To open yourself up to love, use a pink or red sachet filled with rose petals, hibiscus flowers, and a rose quartz heart. Write "I open my heart to love" on a scrap of paper and it tuck in the sachet.

### 11. Fertile Ground

On the new moon, form a phallus of green wax or clay. Place it on top of a Sheela-na-gig image and slip them under your bed as a fertility charm.

### 12. Banish a Pesky Ex

On the dark moon, take a photo of your ex and roll it into a scrap of black cloth. Wrap a black ribbon around it and tie three knots while saying, "Knot one, we're done. Knot two, f#$k you. Knot three, I'm free." Burn it.

### 13. Siren Song Bath Soak

Mix the following ingredients in a large glass bowl and store in a glass container. Use ½ cup per bath. (Makes 5 cups.)

- 3 cups Epsom salt
- 1½ cups coarse Himalayan salt
- ½ cup baking soda
- 2 tablespoons almond oil

- Oils: 10 drops rosemary, 10 drops tuberose, 5 drops vanilla
- 2 tablespoons dried rose petals

### 14. Dream Lover Sachet

Fill a sachet with an herb mix consisting of 1 part mugwort, 1 part rose petal, and ½ part lavender. Place under your pillow to dream of your new love.

### 15. Tantric Touch

Touching purely for pleasure is known as tantric touch. Try this deeply healing and loving experience with a trusted partner while burning Love Is in the Air Incense Blend (recipe next).

### 16. Love Is in the Air Incense Blend

This is a wonderful blend to use during tantric touch or whenever you want to set the mood for love.

- 2 parts sandalwood
- 1 part rose petals
- ½ part cinnamon bark
- A few drops ylang-ylang essential oil

### 17. Love Rocks

Try these gemstones for working love spells:

*Rose quartz:* Love, self-love

*Pink tourmaline:* Acceptance, emotional connection

*Opal:* Amplifies energy, breaks down inhibitions

*Garnet:* Self-confidence, passion

*Moonstone:* Sexuality, arousal, fertility

## Lust

Let go of your inhibitions and enjoy the magickal, sexual being you are. These tips, spells, charms, and recipes are designed to allow you to explore your sexuality with confidence. (Note: Although sexual acts between consenting adults are never wrong, remember it is important to gauge your level of comfort, and know it is always okay to say no.)

### 18. Free Your Fantasies

Meditate in a space where you feel free to explore your sexual fantasies while burning Courageous Sex Incense Blend (recipe next). Use this time to play out sexual scenarios in your mind. How does it make you feel? How do think your partner would feel? Remember, whatever your kink, sexual acts between consenting adults are never wrong.

### 19. Courageous Sex Incense Blend

Burn 2 parts dragon's blood, 1 part cinnamon bark, and ½ part jasmine flowers in a fireproof dish on a charcoal incense tab.

### 20. Hot as F&$k Ritual

Dress up in the hottest little piece of something you own, whether it's sexy lingerie, a leather thong, or something steamy made of latex. Now stand in front of a mirror, and with red lipstick write "Hot as F#$k" across the glass. Say the words until they are embedded within your soul. Take a selfie. Own your sexiness.

### 21. Summoning through Masturbation

You are your most powerful tool. Utilize your sexual energy to feed your intended goal through orgasm. As you come, channel that energy to manifest your intentions.

### 22. Hot Sex Massage Oil

This gently heating massage oil is just the thing to start a night of pleasure out right. Combine the ingredients and pour into a dark glass bottle. Gently shake. This oil has a six-month shelf life, so enjoy often.

- 8 ounces grapeseed oil
- ¼ teaspoon vitamin E oil
- ½ teaspoon vanilla extract
- 8–10 drops ginger essential oil
- 5 drops bergamot essential oil
- 2–4 drops cinnamon essential oil

### 23. Powerful Fluids

Anointing your spell candles with sexual fluids is powerful magick. (Note: Bodily fluids such as blood and semen may carry disease. It is important for you and your partner(s) to be tested before engaging in magick using sexual fluids.)

*Menstrual blood:* Protection, empowerment, fertility, sex, binding

*Urine:* Binding, luck, money, power

*Semen:* Faithfulness, attraction, assertion

*Vaginal fluid:* Binding, attraction, sex

### 24. To Summon a F#$k Boi

On the full moon, light a red phallic candle that has been anointed with vaginal fluid or semen. As you watch the flame dance, visualize the perfect image of your f#$k boi—how they look, dress, pleasure you, etc. Draw them to you. Allow the candle to burn out safely.

## 25. Domme It

Embrace your inner domme. But first, consecrate your tools of pleasure. Before embarking on a night of play, place tools such as whips, collars, handcuffs, sex toys, etc., in a circle of red tea light candles. Lay your hands over them and say, "I call upon (name of lusty god/goddess of your choice) to bless my tools of pleasure. May they stimulate under my sturdy pressure."

## 26. Threesome on My Besom

Are you and your partner desiring a partner for a threesome? Lay three brooms in a triangular formation on the floor. At two corners of your triangle, place white candles that represent you and your partner. Use a candle scribe to draw the planetary symbol for Mars (♂) drawing in sexual energy on a third red candle. Anoint with Dionysus Oil (recipe next) and light the candles. While nude, sit in the middle of the formation with your partner, and as you practice tantric touch, use your combined energies to *draw in* your desired third.

## 27. Dionysus Oil

Use this oil when working magick connected to lust, sexual pleasure, and indulgence. Add the following oils to 8 ounces carrier oil:

- 10 drops oakmoss oil
- 5 drops pine oil
- 3 drops apple oil
- 2 drops cannabis oil*

* Please check your state cannabis regulations for adult use.

### 28. Come Fly with Me Lubricant

Cannabis-based lubricant, when applied to the walls of the vagina and/or anus, increases blood flow and heightens pleasure. Here's how to make your own.

- 4 ounces fractionated coconut oil
- 1 gram cannabis distillate (1:1 recommended)

Heat the fractionated coconut oil in a microwave-safe container for approximately thirty seconds. Warm sealed distillate in a cup of warm water. Empty the distillate into the heated oil and stir until completely dissolved. Transfer to a dark jar. Apply the lubricant twenty minutes before sexual activity to feel the full effects. (Note: This lubricant may cause an allergic reaction, so test before use on the inside of your wrist. If there is any redness, irritation, or swelling, discontinue use. Also, check your state cannabis regulations for adult use.)

### 29. Friends with Benefits Protection Spell

To protect the bond of friendship while exploring sexual pleasure with a friend, burn a mixture of basil, rose petals, and calendula over a charcoal tab. When the ashes are cool, place them in a small jar along with a scrap of paper with the words "friends first—friends forever" written on it. Add two rose quartz hearts and a bit of honey. Secure the jar and seal with red sealing wax. Keep under your bed.

### 30. Slutty as I Wanna Be

We are sexual beings, and as long as a sexual act is done between consenting adults, there is no need for shame. Embrace your sexual freedom and reclaim the word *slut*! Print out the selfie from our Hot as F#$k Ritual and surround it with other sexually liberated images. Light a red candle that has been scribed with the word *slut*. Scream the word aloud and know you are a god/goddess free to express your sexuality however you choose.

### 31. Hex Sexual Shaming

On the night of the dark moon, burn a black candle scribed with hex symbols atop printed images of sexual shaming found on social media, the news, etc. Repeat, "No room for hate." Let the candle burn out safely.

### 32. Stick It to the Prick Spell

Have you ever been ghosted, manipulated, cheated on, or gaslighted by a partner? I think we've all known someone who has acted like a complete prick, leading us to feel self-doubt and threatening our self-esteem. This ritual is designed to help you remember who has the upper hand. During the dark of the moon, form a phallus from wax or clay, then use a nail to carve the person's name into it. Now stab it with as many pins as you like. Place in a jar, fill it with vinegar, and secure the lid. Before throwing it in the trash, spit on it and don't look back.

### 33. Celebration Soak

Celebrate your sexual liberation with this exhilarating bath glitter bomb. Mix the first five ingredients in a large bowl. Pack into bath bomb molds with pockets of glitter. Let dry for five hours before use.

- 1 cup baking soda
- ½ cup Epsom salt
- ½ cup citric acid
- 3 tablespoons fractionated coconut oil
- 10 drops (your favorite) essential oil
- Colorful bath glitter

### 34. It's a Fling Thing

Looking for a hookup? A concoction made of 4 ounces fractionated coconut oil, 10 drops rose oil, 5 drops hibiscus oil, and a little semen or vaginal fluid is just the thing to dab on yourself before heading out on the town. (Note: Bodily fluids such as blood and semen may carry disease. It is important for you and your partner(s) to be tested before engaging in magick using sexual fluids.)

## Life

RuPaul says it best: "If you can't love yourself, how in the hell you gonna love somebody else?" These tips, spells, charms, and recipes were created with self-love in mind.

### 35. Own Your Uniqueness

While burning Lucky to Be Me Incense Blend (recipe next), use a pad and pen to write down ten wonderfully unique facts about yourself. Close your eyes and meditate on your strengths. When you are finished, light a bright yellow candle and repeat, "There is no one quite like me. I am unique. I am lucky. Blessed be."

### 36. Lucky to Be Me Incense Blend

Use this incense blend for the Own Your Uniqueness spell or for any spells for self-love.

- 2 parts dried orange peel
- 1 part rosemary
- ½ part ground nutmeg
- A few drops vanilla essential oil

### 37. Cultivating Confidence

To create a daily visual reminder of your strength and power, dye a raw egg bright orange and use your candle scribe to scratch words of power, symbols, etc., all over it. Plant your egg during a waxing moon phase in a planter and sprinkle forget-me-not seeds. As the flowers grow and bloom, you will be reminded of your growing confidence.

### 38. Give It to the Trees

De-stressing can be as easy as leaning against a tree. To release negative residue picked up throughout your day, lean against a favorite tree. As you do this, close your eyes and feel the tree absorbing all of that bad energy, leaving you refreshed and ready to take on the world.

### 39. Passion Party

Dancing naked under a full moon might seem like a cliché, but I'm telling you, there's nothing like it to get that passionate energy flowing. Try it with a wild drum track or music from your favorite band. Feel the freedom.

### 40. Witch, Know Thyself

As part of a spiritual self-care routine, a weekly simple three-card tarot spread is a great tool for spiritual support (and a great introduction to tarot for beginners).

### 41. Incense Blend for Wisdom

Mix and use this blend in meditation for wisdom and reflection.

- 2 parts dried sage
- 1 part lavender buds
- 1 part sandalwood resin
- ½ part pine resin

### 42. Walk It Out

The grounding effects of a quick walk in the park at lunch or along the trails at your favorite state park on the weekend can do wonders for anyone, physically, emotionally, and spiritually. Make this one a habit.

### 43. Stress Tamer Tea Blend

Combine the following ingredients and add to a tea ball. Let steep for five minutes and enjoy.

- 2 parts chamomile
- 1 part lemon balm
- ½ part lavender

### 44. Speak Your Truth

Our words have power. While standing on an ocean beach, a hill, a mountaintop, or even a chair, face the east (which represents a new dawn) and cry out your goals, dreams, and ambitions. Give your passion power.

### 45. Candle Spell for Personal Growth

Light a green candle during the new moon and surround it with objects that symbolize your growth. Anoint the candle with Action Oil (recipe next) and focus on your personal goals.

### 46. Action Oil

Use this anointing oil in spells to promote action, growth, and transformation. Mix the following ingredients with 8 ounces carrier oil:

- 15 drops spearmint oil
- 5–6 drops geranium oil
- 4 drops coriander oil

### 47. Release by Candlelight

Walk along with the Dark Goddess on the night of the dark moon by the light of only a candle. Make sure your predetermined circle is free of debris. Start at the eastern point and walk widdershins (counterclockwise). Embrace her dark mantle and let her guide you in releasing emotional strife and unhealthy negative self-talk. Let your inner self guide your journey. Stop only when you feel the time is right.

### 48. Just Cleanse It

Enjoy the purifying effects provided by an herb bundle. Clip 6-to-8-inch lengths of garden sage, lavender, or other purifying garden herbs. Lay your bundle on a table and tie twine made of natural fiber at one end. Wrap twine tightly around the length of your bundle and secure at the top. Let dry for at least two weeks before use.

### 49. Follow Your Passion Sachet

Sometimes passion takes us on an adventure. For safe travels, fill a yellow sachet with rosemary, comfrey, and mugwort, plus a blue agate and an Aegishjalmur charm.

### 50. I Am My Own Light Meditation

Find a relaxing place to meditate. Sit in a comfortable position and close your eyes. Envision a light coming from within you and forming a protective bubble around you. As this happens, remind yourself that you are your own light source. Passion in love, lust, and life comes from within.

**Monica Crosson** (*Concrete, WA*) *has been a practicing witch and educator for over thirty years and is a member of* Evergreen Coven. *She is the author of* The Magickal Family *and* Wild Magical Soul *and is a regular contributor to the* Llewellyn *annuals as well as magazines such as* Enchanted Living *and* Witchology.

**Illustrator: M. Kathryn Thompson**

# Reinventing Money Magic: Abundance Beyond Capitalism

*Melissa Tipton*

If you were an alien tasked with figuring out this whole humanity thing and your only source of intel was Instagram, you might reach some interesting conclusions about human spirituality. Whether you found yourself in a social media rabbit hole of witchcraft, New Age teachings, paganism, Hermetic magick, or the wide world of manifestation techniques, chances are you'd see quite a few posts about money (perhaps under the code word *abundance*) and, specifically, how to get more of it.

After further scrolling, you'd be forgiven for walking away with the impression that money is the universe's way of rewarding humans for being "in alignment" or "high vibe" or for successfully freeing ourselves from the shackles of negative beliefs. Think the right thoughts, keep your aura sparkling and magnetic, dissolve limiting beliefs, and *bingo*—you'll soon find yourself swimming in cash. On the flip side, what if you're broke? Well, you must be dragging your energy down with negative thoughts or operating from a place of lack. Better fix that. (Never mind the effects of systemic racism, sexism, transphobia, etc.)

All snark aside, I'm both fascinated and deeply troubled by the prevalence of this type of spiritual money messaging. Space doesn't permit a rundown of the history of this thinking, which is closely aligned with the New Thought movement (the Law of Attraction being a popular offshoot), but these ideas are far from new. Instead, I'd like to explore why these ideas took such a firm root in our collective psyche and offer an approach to money magic that doesn't view the universe as a giant ATM rewarding us for being "spiritual enough."

## Feeling Like You're Enough in a Capitalist System

To tackle the *why* behind the popularity of messaging connecting material wealth and self-worth, we have to consider just how widespread capitalist values are in our modern world. Even if we personally rail against them, we're still living in a culture steeped in the assumption that the more you have, the better. But, you might be thinking, what about the tiny house movement or the Marie Kondo method? These movements are a (welcome) reaction to the dominant ethos of consumption, and their existence demonstrates how far the pendulum has swung in the more-more-more direction. This is the water we've been swimming in since birth, and sure, we can certainly work to question and reverse the assumptions baked into capitalist thinking, but we'd be wise not to discount their wide-ranging influence, particularly on an unconscious level.

Let's take a peek at one of the bedrock principles of capitalism so we can unpack its connection to "spiritual worthiness." Under capitalism, those with more material resources are allotted more influence and decision-making power. With the advent of personal ownership, what might have started out as, "Well, I own this farm, so I get to make the decisions around here," has become conflated with a person's worth, because capitalism links up how much stuff we own with our deep-seated need to feel like we have an impact on the world. And this need isn't merely rooted in vanity. Imagine if *nothing* we said or did had any effect on our lives—in other words, if we had zero influence. That would be excruciatingly frustrating! We need to have a sense that what we do matters on some level, even if that's on the scale of, *when I tip this coffee pot into the mug, out pours the coffee.* It would be impossible to function in or make sense of a world where our actions were entirely disconnected from effects. Basic physics would fall apart without this relationship. Thus, the need to, and the expectation that we *can*, influence our environment is a fundamental quality of existence as we know it, and it's directly tied to the level of meaning we ascribe to our lives.

As social creatures, we're wired to notice who has influence and who doesn't. Consider how many movies revolve around the trope of the in-crowd versus the outcasts. In these stories, the in-crowd's power derives from their influence—other people care what they think. If this wasn't such a deep, archetypal dynamic within the collective psyche, those stories wouldn't be as powerfully relatable as they are, for who among us can resist a satisfying triumph of the underdog, where the tables are turned and influence is claimed by the formerly powerless?

## Influence and the Magic of Making Money

We've painted a picture of the perfect storm a-brewin' when capitalist values collide with the very natural human need to influence our environment. And when this is viewed through the lens of spirituality, it's easy to transpose this influence onto the spiritual realm. Depending on your belief system, you might frame influence in terms of having a close connection to certain deities or spirit guides, living in alignment with the universe, or the ability to cast spells that work. The common thread is that you're able to impact your surroundings—you're able to effect the changes you desire in your life—whether that's happening because the gods are aiding or favoring you, because you're living in divine flow, or because of any other spiritual mechanism to which you subscribe.

**I don't mean to imply that the gods *don't* aid us or that there *isn't* such a thing as divine flow or effective spells—quite the contrary. But I'm very interested in how these beliefs connect to the rampant self-shaming and victim blaming that crops up in spiritual communities if life isn't going the way we'd like.**

I don't mean to imply that the gods *don't* aid us or that there *isn't* such a thing as divine flow or effective spells—quite the contrary. But I'm very interested in how these beliefs connect to the rampant self-shaming and victim blaming that crops up in spiritual communities if life isn't going the way we'd like. Too often, people are quick to ascribe, for instance, their lack of funds to being low vibe or thinking negative thoughts, but these narratives are far from useful. I mean, if shaming and blaming worked, we'd have all successfully shamed and blamed our way to happiness and enlightenment by now, but clearly that's not the case.

To consider another approach to money magic, I'd like to invoke the wise words of Florence Farr of Golden Dawn fame. Farr is quoted in Mary K. Greer's *Women of the Golden Dawn* as saying, "Magic is unlimiting experience." One of the ways we *limit* experience is by linking things that don't, in reality, need to be linked. We might think of these linkages as conditions that have to be met in order for things to work, and the more links we have, the more conditions that must be met. We've been exploring the ways in which capitalism and our innate social wiring have artificially linked influence, self-worth, and material wealth, and if we heed Farr's claim, then these linkages are limiting our magic.

How? Well, if we believe that all of these elements come as a package deal, then we can't experience any of them unless we're experiencing *all* of them. For instance, if I'm not making as much money as I think I should be, then this formula dictates that I can't enjoy a sense of self-worth. Or if I don't possess enough influence, say, in the form of having a bunch of Instagram followers, then I can't enjoy material wealth. Now, if this formula were true, then we'd be tasked with finding a way to succeed within that framework (which is what the majority of people spend their lives trying to do), but the thing is…it's *not* true. For example, there are plenty of people who have a great deal of material wealth but who struggle with self-worth. Clearly, these elements aren't intrinsically linked.

## Questioning the Ego's "Logic"

Our ego loves to connect things, because this simplifies the complexity of life. This can be useful in certain situations, but unfortunately, the ego isn't terribly concerned with whether or not its linkages are accurate, provided they reduce the number of unknowns and help us live to see another day. Said another way, the ego would rather be certain than correct. Even if the belief that "more money = more influence = more self-worth" makes us feel like crap, the ego loves the simplicity of this formula. Instead of dealing with the discomfort of not knowing how to control things, the ego has a ready answer for our problems. If we don't have enough money, then the ego supplies the reason that this is because we clearly aren't worthy enough and/or don't have enough influence. The message we receive is that people don't care about what we think, or we're just not good enough so why bother trying. And if we're spiritually minded, our reasons get filtered through that lens: we're not spiritual enough or high vibe enough, our manifestation abilities are out of whack, and so on.

Unfortunately, the ego's reasoning often doesn't help us cultivate a magically efficacious mindset. It's hard to tap into your creative problem-solving abilities to, for instance, promote that amazing new product you've created when you're swamped with doubts around your worth as a human being or believe that you deserve to be broke because your vibes are bad. Not to mention, you're more likely to miss viable solutions because they don't fit within the ego's narrow scope. For example, if you're convinced that your lack of funds is due to negativity in your aura, then you might not consider the option of asking for a raise or running an ad to promote your new class. To be clear, I'm not suggesting that you can't or shouldn't do things to improve the health of your aura, but

**I'm not suggesting that you can't or shouldn't do things to improve the health of your aura, but frequently those magical actions will be enhanced by pairing them with "mundane" strategies, such as asking your boss for a raise after you've cleansed your aura.**

frequently those magical actions will be enhanced by pairing them with "mundane" strategies, such as asking your boss for a raise after you've cleansed your aura.

Returning to Farr's quote, "Magic is unlimiting experience," the ego's "reasoning" effectively limits our experience to a narrow subset of options. So I propose a little housecleaning, where we stop asking money to jump through so many hoops in order to enter our lives. Magic, like water, tends to find the path of least resistance. And if we've cluttered that path with countless prerequisites, then like water flowing through a complicated network of clogged pipes, our magic will take longer to manifest; and when or if it finally does, it's often a mere trickle of its former self, before it had to negotiate our energetic obstacle course. This isn't a question of the universe rewarding or punishing us; it's just cause and effect.

## Opening to an Easy Flow of Money

Here's a quick ritual to unlimit your experience of money, opening new pathways for wealth to enter your life. You'll need a piece of paper and a pen, a pair of scissors, and a jar or container. You're welcome to cast a magic circle or establish sacred space however you like. Then write on the paper what you believe is required in order for you to have the level of material wealth you desire. These can be actions you'd need to take, qualities you'd need to possess (such as more confidence), knowledge you'd need to have (such as how to invest)—whatever comes to mind.

Now take a few moments to center yourself, focusing on your breath, closing your eyes, and increasing your sense of being present in your body, right here, right now. In this state, say three times, "My relationship to money is easy and joyful." Finish with, "And so it is!"

Open your eyes and use the scissors to cut out your requirements so that each one now exists on its own little piece of paper. As you cut, focus on the intention that you are unlinking these conditions, making it possible for money to flow without meeting all of these requirements. Place the paper slips in your jar or container, hold it in your hands, and visualize it filling with divine light as you intend that these elements be infused with the organizing harmony of divine energy.

In the days to come, whenever you feel blocked around money, shake up the jar and use it as a divination tool. Ask to be shown which elements have been artificially linked to your money flow by your ego, and pull one or more slips from the jar as your intuition dictates. If, say, you pull "need more confidence," and you've been debating whether or not to host a webinar to promote a new course, you might get the intuitive hit that you've been putting off doing this promotion until you feel more confident, because your ego has set this up as a false requirement. With that insight, you might choose to move forward with the webinar anyway, knowing that you don't *have* to feel confident in order for it to be successful. In fact, we often build confidence by doing things we didn't think we could and proving our ego wrong.

By unlinking elements within our money-making flow, we unlimit how money is able to enter our lives while dismantling the capitalist tether between our bank account and our innate human value. Here's to the magic of unlimiting your experiences!

## References


Greer, Mary K. *Women of the Golden Dawn: Rebels and Priestesses.* Rochester, VT: Park Street Press, 1995.



**Melissa Tipton** *is a Jungian Witch, Structural Integrator, and founder of the Real Magic Mystery School, where she teaches online courses in Jungian Magic, a potent blend of ancient magical techniques and modern psychological insights. She's the author of* Living Reiki: Heal Yourself and Transform Your Life *and* Llewellyn's Complete Book of Reiki. *Learn more and take a free class at www.realmagic.school.*

**Illustrator: Tim Foley**

# Altar Creation: Be Your Own Spiritual Architect

*Michelle Skye*

The clouds are gray overhead as the car rumbles down the busy road. Neon lights glare as a soft rain drums on the windshield. I don't know where I'm going. Not really. I only have an address and a general direction in my mind. I pass through the green light and there, on my right, between an empty lot and a mom-and-pop jewelry store, is a tiny nondescript building with white peeling paint. I enter through the blue door and am greeted with a display of colorful candles, a plethora of herbal wands, and

a cabinet of magical pendants. I wander around searching for... what? Enlightenment, I guess. Wisdom. Knowledge. A friendly voice.

A woman with long, curly hair and swinging skirts greets me from across the room. She is busy. I meander around the tiny store trying to muster the courage to speak. After fifteen minutes and three circles around the shop (it was very small), I approach the woman and ask her about first steps to take in beginning a Pagan practice. Her eyes narrow; she is busy crafting items to sell. After assessing me for a moment (which felt like hours), she suggests that I create an altar.

My mind recoils at this idea. After all, altars are for churches. They're big, with large statues and tons of candles. I cannot fathom where I would find the space for such a creation in my tiny one-bedroom apartment. I immediately reject the woman's idea and hurry outside. Back in the safety of my car, I speed out of the parking lot for home, completely discarding the idea of an altar.

This is a true story. And I'm here to admit that my younger self was wrong. Altars do not have to be big, imposing structures. They do not need to be filled with hundreds of candles. Altars can be anywhere, not just inside a church.

## How to Begin

There is a reason that we generally equate altars with churches. Altars are portals to the Divine, so it makes sense that you would find one in a spiritual center. An impressive altar, massive windows, rising steeples, tolling bells, a religious symbol (or two), and possibly even a graveyard equate, in many people's minds, to a religious location. Name it what you will—church, synagogue, temple—but spirituality is an inherent aspect of these buildings. These days things are more flexible and you can find religious locations in less traditional buildings. Spiritual centers spring up in strip malls, in outdoor tented areas, and even in buildings with stadium seating, complete with giant monitors and state-of-the-art sound systems. But they are still considered religious centers because people gather there to worship, in some form or another. And nine times out of ten, they have an altar.

An altar is a section of a spiritual place that is specifically set aside to access the Divine. Often it houses religious relics, sacred texts, spiritual icons, and items necessary to celebrate the religious experience with the congregation. The altar is typically the focal point of a church (or temple), as the congregation faces it when they file into the pews, benches, or chairs. In fact, the altar is seen as part of, yet separate from, the worshippers, as only certain people are granted access to it. (Sometimes altars are separated by doors, gates, or railings to accentuate their status as being a divine place in a mundane world.)

Considering all the cultural history, not to mention the social and emotional human connection to altars, it's no wonder that modern Pagans choose to include them in their spiritual practice. So how do you begin to create your own altar? You might choose to research altars by reading books and visiting churches and temples in your town, or perhaps by casually dropping hints and posing questions to friends and experts. Artists may gain inspiration from beautiful images online or in magazines. While all this might be helpful, you still may feel overwhelmed by the whole idea of creating a divine location, a portal for spirituality to enter your life. But it doesn't have to be that way.

## Types of Altars

The first step is to decide what kind of altar you want to create. In my experience, there are three distinct types of Pagan altars: the dedication altar, the seasonal altar, and the working altar. Each one serves a different purpose, but they are all equally powerful and sacred.

### Dedication Altar

This type of altar focuses on a specific deity, group of deities, spiritual guide, or sacred entity. Traditionally it does not change very much once it has been set up, although some individuals may add or subtract items as they wish. Candles and incense are often burned on these altars during times of prayer, introspection, or meditation as the practitioner seeks the blessing and guidance of the Divine or gives thanks to Spirit. These altars focus on a long-term connection to the Divine. Examples of dedication altars include an ancestor altar, a healing altar, an altar to Freya (Norse goddess of passion and daring), or an altar to the ancient Egyptian gods.

### Seasonal Altar

This type of altar focuses on the seasons and the sabbats that follow the Wheel of the Year. It is transitory and always changing, just as nature is always shifting and changing. This altar helps practitioners connect to the rhythm of nature. It focuses on the gifts of each season in connection with the eight sabbats or whatever holidays hold significance for the dedicant. Examples of seasonal altars include a New Year's Eve wishing altar, a Samhain/Halloween/Day of the Dead altar, a harvest altar, and a new moon altar.

### Working Altar

This type of altar is created for a specific magical working or ceremonial intent. Magical tools, spell elements, and activation items are the main components of this altar. It is meant to be set up and taken down within the confines of the spell or ceremony. Examples of working altars include a manifestation altar to get a new job, a love altar to energize your second chakra, and a Bast goddess altar to request healing and protection for a beloved animal companion.

## Location, Location, Location

Once you've decided on the type of altar you wish to create, you need to decide where you want it to be located. Altars can be created anywhere! The dusty windowsill in your study can be an altar. The unused end table that only collects random receipts can be an altar. A drawer in your bureau, an unused toy chest, an empty shoebox, or a corner of your garden can all be altars. Here are two unusual suggestions.

### Shoebox Diorama Altar

Turn a shoebox on its side so the inside is facing you and the shortest sides are on the ends. Place it on top of a bureau, TV stand, or shelf. Decorate the inside of the box for whatever purpose you have in mind. You may choose to glue pictures or place stickers inside. (If you are focusing on one deity, pictures related to that deity would be perfect.) You could also paint the inside of your altar or use scrapbook paper to create a beautiful neutral background. Find related miniature magical items to focus your intent. I love shopping online and in person at dollhouse stores for just this purpose. You can find mini brooms (or besoms), fireplaces, chalices, and even chain saws (for cutting those negative energetic cords!). You can also find miniature magical elements in nature, such as bird feathers, flowers, herbs, etc. If this is a working altar, decorate and save the lid so you can close up your shoebox altar after every magical and ceremonial working. With the lid securely in place, you can store it in a secret location.

### Window Altar

Windows are fabulous places for altars because they are inherently magical, being in a liminal space, both inside and outside at the same time. Once you've decided on the focus for your altar, think about what you could hang from the curtain rod (if you have one). Drying herbs lend a decidedly witchy flair to a window altar. You could also hang colorful ribbons, small goddess flags, depictions of the chakras, large feathers, or anything that corresponds to your vision. On the glass panes themselves, consider coloring and taping pictures from stained-glass coloring books with magical or nature-based drawings. Your energy will be added to the altar through your creativity! Finally, the windowsill is a completely blank slate for you to add your treasures. Crystals, seashells, a goddess statue (or two), or a magic wand would all fit beautifully in this skinny space at the base of your altar. Keep in mind that a window is a place that is often in motion. Wind, rain, curtains, and privacy blinds can move your altar items, sometimes with disastrous results. For this reason, I recommend using sturdy wooden statues and choosing crystals and stones where you won't mind if they end up with a chip or two.

## Create a Moon Altar

If you're lucky enough to have space for a traditional altar in your home (such as an end table or a nightstand), you'll want to build your divine creation from the bottom up. In other words, you need to start thinking about purpose, color, deities, spiritual beings, and magical items. Let's see how this all flows together with the example of a moon altar.

Moon altars are very traditional Pagan altars, partly because they are so incredibly useful. A moon altar can be three altars in one: a devotional altar to a specific moon goddess or god or to the planetary body herself; a seasonal altar as the moon shifts throughout the month and has different names throughout the year; and a working altar since the moon is often associated with magic and spellcasting. You can do anything related to magic at your multifunctional moon altar!

As with any altar, you need to start with an altar cloth. This is a piece of material that sets the stage for all the other items you're going to add to your altar. You can find beautiful Pagan-themed altar cloths online or at most New Age stores, but you can also use mundane items from around your home. A tablecloth folded up small, a decorative scarf, or even a blanket can be used as an altar cloth. Some of my favorite altar cloths have come from thrift stores and rummage sales. Sometimes I go to my local fabric store and purchase a half yard of material to use. For our moon altar, I'm going to choose a piece of dark material with a celestial scene on it—moons, stars, sparkles.

**A tablecloth folded up small, a decorative scarf, or even a blanket can be used as an altar cloth. Some of my favorite altar cloths have come from thrift stores and rummage sales.**

Now you need a focal piece for your altar. This could be either a god or goddess statue or a large picture that has vertical height. You're going to place this in the center of your altar. It will be the item that immediately draws your eye every time you work at your altar, so make sure you really love it! For your moon altar, you may decide on a statue of Selene or Luna or a moon fairy. You can keep the same statue up for the entire year or switch it to reflect the lunar phases or the monthly energies of the yearly moons. Here are some ideas:

- January (Wolf Moon)—Add a statue of Skadi, Norse goddess of snow, might, and feminine power.
- February (Snow Moon)—Place handcrafted snowflakes decorated with silver glitter around a snow globe of two lovers in a winter scene.
- March (Worm Moon)—Borrow the children's book *Diary of a Worm* by Doreen Cronin from the library and, after reading it (it's very funny), use it as your focal point for the month.

- April (Pink Moon)—Gather branches from your flowering trees, or purchase some pink flowers and enjoy their beautiful scent.
- May (Flower Moon)—Add more flowers and maybe also a picture of the Roman goddess Flora, whose holy festival was traditionally celebrated in late April to early May.
- June (Strawberry Moon)—A Strawberry Shortcake doll is a no-brainer for this month if you enjoy a little whimsy. Her ideals of community and cooperation are perfect for emerging from winter isolation.
- July (Buck Moon)—Add statues of the Wiccan Lunar Goddess and Horned God to embody the energies of this warm, passionate moon.
- August (Sturgeon Moon)—The moon goddess Artemis, with her movement and vigor, is a perfect complement to the running of the fish, as they return to their ancestral lakes to spawn.
- September (Harvest Moon)—Take some dried wheat and grasses and spray-paint them silver. Place them in a dark blue vase for added drama.
- October (Blood Moon)—Tap into the power of Hecate, the crone goddess of magic, by adding a statue or picture of her to aid in connecting with the powerful energies of this moon.
- November (Frost Moon)—Tack some beautiful woolen mittens above your altar and reconnect with the stately presence of Lady Luna.
- December (Oak Moon)—The Oak King is taking his last breaths as he prepares to battle the Holly King at the Winter Solstice. Add some oak leaves edged in silver glitter for a fitting tribute.

Once you've secured your focal point for the month, add items of power to your altar, making sure they connect to your overall goal and purpose. These can be crystals, herbs, small figurines, flowers or vegetation, jewelry, and sigils or symbols. You may also choose to add some (or all) of your magical tools, such as your wand, athame, pentacle, chalice, censer, etc. Since your magical tools hold power for you to manifest and shape your life, you'll probably want to leave them on your altar for short periods of time. If you do choose to keep them on your altar indefinitely, make sure you cleanse them periodically with salt water, incense, or quartz crystals.

For our moon altar, some power items might be moonstones, quartz crystals of any shape, and snow quartz. These stones resonate with the energy of the moon. You can also use white stones that you find out in nature. Burning a wand of purifying herbs will help you cleanse your altar every time you sit or stand before it. White, silver, or black candles can be used to honor the gods, goddesses, and the celestial moon herself. The candles can also be used in spellwork.

Consider adding small figurines of animals with white fur, such as arctic hares and foxes, snowy owls, and white horses. The possibilities are endless and can be found at many craft stores for a very reasonable price. Anything that connects you to the moon, such as silver glitter, star constellations, or silver jewelry, can also take up residence on your altar. I often place glitter in a small bowl. When I stop to take a moment in front of my altar to center, I sprinkle a small amount of glitter on the altar and on myself as well to connect to the energies of the Divine.

When placing these smaller items on the altar, create a pattern that is pleasing to the eye. Humans typically resonate with symmetrical, balanced arrangements, with similar colors and shapes forming designs on either side of the main focal piece. Don't be afraid to switch things around to see what you like. Altars are meant to be fluid, as they connect to you and your relationship with the Divine. You may decide that you always need a candle on your altar, or perhaps you don't feel right without a pentacle representation. There is no wrong way to craft a sacred space as long as you're listening to your heart.

. . . . . . . . . . . . .

Crafting an altar is an art form, and viewing the altar space as a blank canvas can help to remove the internal expectations that we place on ourselves. As we explore the artistic elements of color, shape, balance, and design, we tap into our own divinity. We lose ourselves in the moment, and at the end of the experience we have a beautiful altar to gaze at and use for our magical intent. Above all, creating your altar should be fun, as it is an expression of your love and devotion to the Divine. If it feels like work, then step back, take a few moments to breathe, and ask the Divine to guide your hands to the ideas, items, and magical elements that will most benefit you (and them!) at this moment in time.

**Michelle Skye** *is a dedicated tree-hugging, magic-wielding, goddess-loving Pagan. While she is best known for her three goddess books,* Goddess Alive!, Goddess Afoot!, *and* Goddess Aloud!, *she also works closely with many gods and male magic practitioners. Michelle is fond of reading (a lot!), rainbows, crows, oracle decks, walks in the woods, Middle Eastern dance, spellwork, grunge music, silver jewelry (especially if it's sparkly), and quirky '80s movies. She creates crafts and spells with her magic circle, the Crafty Witches, and celebrates the sabbats with her family coven at home. She has been spinning magic into the world her whole life but has been following the Pagan path for just over twenty years.*

**Illustrator: Bri Hermanson**

# Herbs for Prosperity

*Elizabeth Barrette*

The search for material needs is among the most popular topics in magic. People want wealth, money, a career, good business, financial security, and success. Magic offers a way to go beyond the practical steps toward prosperity. Many herbs are associated with money. They can be used at home, at work, in food, in magic, and many other ways. Take a look at some of the most popular prosperity plants and what you can do with them.

## Prosperity Herbs

Many money-drawing herbs are things you can grow at home. Others you'll probably need to purchase. They range from small plants to large trees. The leaves are usually used, but also the roots, flowers, or seeds at times. Energy matters, so choose plants grown for magical use if possible.

### Alfalfa

Alfalfa (*Medicago sativa*) is a legume commonly grown in pastures. You can therefore get it cheaply, but alfalfa grown for magical uses will pack more punch. It reaches about knee-high and produces pretty purple flowers. It is ruled by Venus and Earth. Growing it near the home protects against hunger and poverty. Fill a small jar with alfalfa hay and keep it in a kitchen cabinet to welcome abundance. If you make potpourri, you can also use the dried flowers. Scattering alfalfa ash around a business maintains wealth and prosperity. A sachet at work brings good fortune in professional endeavors. As an herb, alfalfa is highly nutritious, whether used in tea or soup or as sprouts in a sandwich.

### Basil

Basil (*Ocimum basilicum*) is a sweet, spicy herb that grows between knee and hip height. Other variants include holy basil (*Ocimum sanctum*) and lemon basil (*Ocimum × citriodorum*). It is ruled by Mars and fire. Basil attracts money and wealth and promotes harmony and love. Use dried basil in sachets or incense. Place whole dried leaves in the cash register to encourage sales. Grow basil plants near the door to attract customers to a business. The woody stems can be used to make beads. Basil oil can be used in sprays or floor washes. Holy basil can encourage religious donations. Widely used in cooking, basil offers many options for cakes and ale in a prosperity ritual; pesto is especially popular because nuts and olive oil relate to wealth also. Wear a garland of basil leaves during such rituals. To save money, make a money-drawing box of olive or pecan wood. Anoint it with a prosperity oil, write your intention on a piece of paper in the box, fill it with dried basil leaves, and start your collection with a ten dollar bill. This will make it easier to save money.

### Buckeye

Buckeye (*Aesculus* spp.) is also known as horse chestnut or conker. This tall, attractive tree produces lovely flowers followed by glossy brown nuts with a distinctive pale spot on top. Native species support wildlife from hummingbirds to squirrels, making it good for "give and get back" types of magic. While the nuts are toxic, there is a peanut butter and chocolate candy called "buckeyes" due to the resemblance, which you can use in the cakes and ale portion of a prosperity ritual. Buckeye is ruled by Jupiter and fire. It is used for money drawing and healing. Carry a buckeye to bring good luck and success, or wrap it in a dollar bill and put it in a brown sachet to attract money. The game of Conkers is played by stringing buckeyes on thread and swinging them together until one breaks; a winning conker absorbs more magical energy from the nuts it breaks.

### Chamomile

Chamomile (*Anthemis nobilis*) is an herb with fine, frilly leaves and daisylike flowers. German chamomile (*Matricaria recutita*) has similar traits and uses. It is ruled by the Sun and water. Most people know this as an herb for relaxing tea. For prosperity work, it is the bright golden centers of the flowers that help attract wealth. Stuff them into a sachet of gold or yellow cloth to promote prosperity. You can also sniff the herb to reduce money worries. Another approach is to add the flowers to potpourri, especially in a business for calm financial transactions. Chamomile tea or beer can be used for cakes and ale in a prosperity ritual.

### Devil's Shoestring

Devil's Shoestring (*Viburnum alnifolium, Viburnum* spp.) is a stringy type of honeysuckle relative that grows in much of North America and is often considered a weed. It is ruled by Mercury and fire. It is good for employment, luck, and protection against evil. This is particularly helpful for warding off toxic bosses or coworkers. Carry a piece to get a job or resolve problems at work. Place it in your wallet or purse to attract money. Add it to a jar of other protective herbs and keep in your home to block curses, especially those aimed at financial ruin. You can make a blended anointing oil with pecan or olive oil, a piece of Devil's Shoestring, and a Lucky Hand. Allow the mixture to sit for a few days, then use it to anoint candles or yourself for employment, protection, or gambling luck.

### High John the Conqueror Root

High John the Conqueror root (*Ipomoea purga*) is a type of morning glory with pink to purple flowers. It can be grown as a perennial in warm climates or an annual in cold climates. Like most vines, it needs support for climbing, so give it a trellis or wire fence. It is ruled by Mars and fire. High John promotes money, success, happiness, and love. Because it is associated with a slave who won freedom through trickery, it is good for tricksters in general and escaping bondage or bad bosses in particular. The root can be carried alone or added to a mojo bag to attract wealth and affection. It also blocks curses and breaks hexes. To make anointing oil for candles, soak chopped roots and a silver coin in mineral oil for one moon cycle.

### Lucky Hand

Lucky Hand (*Orchis* spp.) is also known as Helping Hand or Hand of Power. It comes from an orchid plant and is thus usually purchased rather than grown. It is ruled by Venus and water. Magically, Lucky

Hand attracts money, employment, luck, and protection. It can be used whole or powdered and mixed with other magical materials. People often carry the whole roots for luck at interviews. It is added to mojo bags or witch jars for extra strength, often with a lodestone for more drawing power. The powder can be blended into money-drawing incense. It is sprinkled on money or lottery tickets. It may be added to a bath, floor wash, or laundry. To make Lucky Hand oil, soak a whole hand root in essential oil, which may then be used to anoint candles, people, or work tools. Complementary herbs include five-finger grass and High John the Conqueror root to attract money, luck, and success. Combine them in a green bag for power and wealth.

### Orange Mint

Orange mint (*Mentha citrata*) is also known as bergamot mint. It has square stems and grows about knee-high; its leaves give off a minty, citrusy scent. Like most mints, it is easy to grow and spreads readily, so you might want to keep it in a container. It is ruled by Mercury and air. Tuck a leaf into a checkbook or other financial book to draw money and success. It also works in wallets, purses, and sachets. This is one of the best herbs for career magic, so a yellow sachet works well for that. Rub fresh leaves on your hands or money before buying things to encourage the money to return. This works especially well when you shop locally, to keep money in the community. Add to baths or soaps relating to prosperity, as the uplifting scent gives energy. The essential oil can be used for personal scents, aromatherapy, or massage. As an herb, the leaves make tasty tea, especially when combined with black tea.

### Patchouli

Patchouli (*Pogostemon cablin*) has fuzzy green leaves and grows between knee and hip height. It is ruled by Saturn and earth. Patchouli attracts money and prosperity. If you have nightmares about poverty or debt, a dream pillow with patchouli may encourage better dreams. It offers protection and banishes harmful people or energies. Patchouli can make you seem more attractive in general. It grants courage in financial endeavors. Sprinkle some in your wallet or purse to attract money. It is widely used in prosperity incense and oil. The essential oil is used for skin care and massage blends.

### Pecan

Pecan (*Carya illinoinensis*) is a type of hickory tree with large, sweet nuts. It grows up to seventy-five feet high and can fruit for three hundred years. It is ruled by Mercury and air. Pecan assists with money, employment, and prosperity. Grown in the yard, it promotes wealth and financial stability. Because pecans were used in trading, they assist business deals; keep a bowl of them in the office. Unripe pecans can be fermented for cold dyeing, which results in a rich brown color ideal for sachets in earth or prosperity magic. Pecan oil makes a great base for anointing oil in money spells. Shelled pecans are used to make pralines and pecan pie, two excellent options for cakes and ale in rituals relating to wealth.

### Sage

Sage (*Salvia*) is a genus of small woody shrubs spanning both culinary and ornamental species. Its size ranges from about knee-high to over head-high depending on species. Garden sage (*Salvia officinalis*) has many cultivars, such as golden garden sage (*Salvia officinalis* 'Icterina'), with green and gold leaves; purple garden sage (*Salvia officinalis* 'Purpurea'), with purple leaves; and tricolor sage (*Salvia officinalis* 'Tricolor'), with leaves of variegated cream, green, and pink. Ornamentals include scarlet sage (*Salvia splendens*) and pineapple sage (*Salvia elegans*), with red flowers; Blue Queen (*Salvia × superba*), with navy to blue-violet flowers; Victoria sage (*Salvia farinacea*), with purple or white flowers; and Point Sal sage (*Salvia leucophylla*), with pink pom-pom flowers. Sage is the most popular herb for cleansing, whether loose leaves or sticks. Burn it to purify a home or business and before prosperity rituals. Whole sage leaves dried flat can symbolize money.

## Feng Shui and Prosperity

If you follow feng shui, there are three sectors in your garden ideal for growing prosperity herbs. The two directions ruled by wood are east and southeast. As the southeast is also the "wealth and luck" sector, this is the best position for a prosperity garden if feasible. The south direction is ruled by fire; if it is weak, then adding wood will strengthen it.

Create subtle, flowing paths for the chi energy to follow. A wavy border or an herb spiral are good examples. Straight lines can allow the energy to flow too fast and cause problems. Choose decorations that enhance your goals. For example, golden balls floating in a fountain support the money and abundance energy of the southeast. A piece of bamboo or other wooden furniture in the south will support the fire energy there. So will herbs with red or purple colors, such as many sages have.

**Create subtle, flowing paths [in your garden] for the chi energy to follow. A wavy border or an herb spiral are good examples. Straight lines can allow the energy to flow too fast and cause problems.**

Much the same applies to the directions inside your house, with potted plants or sachets instead of a whole garden. Use round or oval pots to make a container garden on a porch or in a sunny window.

Create a cluster in your home office to attract wealth. Place a plant at the end of a hallway to counteract the sha chi so that straight-running energy doesn't make trouble.

## Grow a Prosperity Garden

Begin planning a prosperity garden with the largest feature. If you would like a tree, such as buckeye or pecan, then position that first. Fill in the other plants around it. (If you already have a tree, you will have to work around it wherever it is.) Because plants need sunlight, gardens are often designed facing the sun, with the shorter plants in front and taller ones in back. However, people also like to plant gardens around a tree. This can work if you put the sun-loving plants toward the outside of the area and the shade-loving plants closer to the tree. Jupiter's distaff sage (*Salvia glutinosa*) grows in deep, dry shade under trees. Orchids like Lucky Hand are jungle plants and like moderate to deep shade. Chamomile prefers part shade. Basil and mint will tolerate some shade. Many sages are sun-lovers.

Make sure you can reach everything in your garden. Plants should not be more than arm's-length from where you will be standing. A long bed is easier to reach than a large round one, although an herb spiral works too. If you make a keyhole garden, which has a C-shape so you can get inside it, then you can place a stepping stone in the center with a money-drawing emblem on it—or just paint the thing gold like a coin.

Many prosperity herbs grow to about knee height and do well together, such as basil, chamomile, orange mint, patchouli, and sage. However, some sages get quite a lot bigger, so you may want to use those on their own, as specimen plants. Alfalfa also gets about knee-high but does better in a bed of its own; treat it like a patch of shaggy lawn and let the wildlife enjoy it. High John the Conqueror root is a type of morning glory, so it needs something to climb, such as a trellis. Look for one with a gold tone or prosperity symbolism, or hang a money emblem at the top.

## Spells, Charms, and Artifacts

Prosperity herbs can be used in many different types of magic. As you've already seen, these applications are often quick and easy. However, you can also use more complex workings to increase the power.

### Prosperity Candle Spell

For this spell you need a green seven-knob wishing candle, a safe candleholder, a lighter, and any seven prosperity herbs. The herbs can be fresh or dried, or you can use essential oil. The spell takes seven days to cast, and you should do it before an important money event like applying for a mortgage. On the first day, rub the top knob with one prosperity herb and light the candle. Then concentrate on your need for wealth and say:

*Money, money, come to me,*
*Over land and over sea.*
*Bring enough for all my needs,*
*Money growing just like seeds.*

Let the candle burn until the first knob is consumed, then put it out. The next day, rub the second knob with the second herb. Say the words and again let the knob burn down. Repeat the process with the remaining knobs. On the seventh day, allow the candle to burn down entirely—some of them have a base below the knob. If any scraps remain, bury them in a hole near your home.

### Money Nuts

For this charm you need one buckeye and one pecan in the shell, plus some gold crochet thread or craft string. If you can knit or crochet, use that to make a tiny net bag around each nut, then connect them with a short string in the middle. If not, you can just tie four threads together and knot them around each nut like making a fishnet, then connect them from the tops. As you work, say, "Knots never come free; I bind money to me." Use the central connecting thread to hang your money nuts wherever you need prosperity, such as over the desk where you pay bills. Then say, "Wealth come to the money nuts with no ifs, ands, or buts."

### High John's Lucky Shoestring Charm

To make this good luck charm, you need a hand-size piece of green cloth and some gold sewing thread. The power is provided by a magnet, a coin, a piece of High John the Conqueror root, a Lucky Hand, and a bit of Devil's Shoestring. First put the magnet on the cloth, then the coin, then the herbs. Use the gold thread to sew or tie the bundle closed. Carry the good luck charm whenever your wealth depends on luck, such as entering a raffle or lottery.

### Money Soap

At a craft store, buy glycerin soap base, green coloring, and a coin-shaped mold. (If you can't find a coin mold, you can just drop a coin into a plain mold.) You also need essential oil or dried herbs from one to three of the following: basil, chamomile, orange mint, patchouli, and sage. Dried herbs need to be powdered. Follow the package instructions to melt the glycerin base. Add a small amount of dried herbs or essential oil. Add 1 to 2 drops of green coloring. Pour the melted soap into the mold, then set it in a cool place to harden. Wash with your money soap before a prosperity ritual or job interview.

Prosperity comes from many sources but is primarily associated with the element of earth. Herbs, which grow in the earth, naturally absorb this energy. By growing your own prosperity herbs and/or learning to use them in magical workings, you can direct that energy for your own benefit. Life is certainly much easier with a little extra luck bringing money your way.

**Elizabeth Barrette** *has been involved with the Pagan community for more than thirty-two years. She served as the managing editor of* PanGaia *for eight years and the dean of studies at the Grey School of Wizardry for four years. She has written columns on beginning and intermediate Pagan practice, Pagan culture, and Pagan leadership. Her book* Composing Magic: How to Create Magical Spells, Rituals, Blessings, Chants, and Prayers *explains how to combine writing and spirituality. She lives in central Illinois, where she has done much networking with Pagans in her area, such as coffeehouse meetings and open sabbats. Her other public activities include Pagan picnics and science fiction conventions. She enjoys magical crafts, historical religions, and gardening for wildlife. Her other writing fields include speculative fiction, gender studies, and social and environmental issues. Visit her blog* The Wordsmith's Forge *(https://ysabetwordsmith.dreamwidth.org) or website* PenUltimate Productions *(http://penultimateproductions.weebly.com). Her coven site, which includes extensive Pagan materials, is* Greenhaven: A Pagan Tradition *(http://greenhaventradition.weebly.com).*

**Illustrator: Bri Hermanson**

# Witchcraft Essentials

Practices, Rituals & Spells

# Flower Magic: Talking with Plants

Charlie Rainbow Wolf

When I was working the psychic circuit back in the 1990s, a lady came into the venue one night to do a flower sentience. I'd been making herbal preparations and kitchen cosmetics for well over a decade, but I'd never heard of a flower sentience! That night opened my eyes to understand that flowers and foliage don't just have a purpose; they have a presence as well. There's a language they speak, and I've never seen them in quite the same light since I opened myself to that awareness.

My love affair with flora began in the 1970s. I was a young bride living on a farm in rural Lincolnshire, and I borrowed Jeanne Rose's *Herbs & Things* from the mobile library. From that moment, I was hooked. My kitchen was soon full of soap experiments, infusions, tinctures, salves, and decoctions—some more successful than others! It wasn't until I saw that guest at the psychic venue actually talking with the flowers on that fateful Friday night that I began to see how everything pieced together into a much bigger picture.

Now that I've got my own postage stamp of land here in South Central Illinois, I feel I've gone full circle from the young maiden experimenting with what she foraged from the fields to the old crone who plants things deliberately and lets the indigenous plants of the garden teach her. Everything is so intricately connected; it just takes a willingness to learn, and nature will comply.

## The Language of Flowers

So just how do flowers "speak"? I don't think there is really any one way. For example, I was making a healing bundle for someone with arthritis once. It was nearly there, but something was lacking. I sat out in the autumnal sun to think about what was missing, and I spied a fern growing in a shaded corner. I don't recall ever having read anything about fern as a remedy for arthritis, yet when I gave thought to how the fern grows, I knew I had the right plant. Its fronds slowly and deliberately unfurl and open, much the same as my intent for my friend's arthritic fingers.

Another way I have conversed with flowers in the past is to use one of the many flower oracles on the market. My initial doorway into this language was with Michael Tierra's *Herbal Tarot*, and while I appreciated it, the cards did not always resonate with how I perceived the plants. There are many plant oracles on the market now, and I've peeked at most of them! The two that have resonated with me the strongest and stayed with me the longest are Marlene Rudginsky's *The Flower Speaks* and Carr-Gomm's *The Druid Plant Oracle.*

When it comes to understanding the language of flowers, I take advantage of books, too. My go-to for looking at their magical properties has to be Scott Cunningham and his *Encyclopedia of Magical Herbs.* It's a tried-and-true classic and I heartily recommend it as being a very good book, but it's not the only book on my shelf when it comes to speaking with herbs and flowers. Accompanying it are Jill Davies's *A Garden of Miracles*, Cicely Mary Barker's *The Complete Book of the Flower Fairies*, and more. All of these add some *oomph* to the information, but to really give my work some welly, I focus on what the plant is saying to me at that time. People have many facets, and so do plants and flowers. The rose has thorns that prick and protect as well as a scent that seduces and romances. It's still the same flower.

**People have many facets, and so do plants and flowers. The rose has thorns that prick and protect as well as a scent that seduces and romances. It's still the same flower.**

Having said that, there are some blanket observations that are helpful when it comes to learning to speak the language of flowers in order to add them to magical practices. I'm big into blending my own loose incense and making my own herbal bath preparations (salts and soaps being my favorites), and I use flowers in many forms, from their dried leaves and petals, to their crushed roots, to essential oils made from their vitality. Some I gather from the garden and others I purchase from a reputable online supplier where I know they are food-grade quality and responsibly harvested. Intent is the main ingredient; everything else just adds focus and energy.

I've used *flowers* as a sweeping term in this article, because it's not just the flower heads that are used for magical purposes. Looking at roses, for example, I use the flower petals of course, but I also sometimes use the thorns in witch bottles and the hips in infusions and decoctions. The catmint plant has a beautiful mauve flower, but I have found that the young spring leaves add the most effective properties to my endeavors. I start any work by examining my desired outcome, then do a bit of soul-searching as to why I want this to happen. Next I arm myself with my reference materials and calculate what I need to get that result.

## Magical Flowers

For space reasons, I've chosen a few of my favorite flowers here—the ones I use often in my incense and herbal preparations—and the main ways that I use them. These are the ones I pick in my yard and garden, the ones that know my name. They're pretty widespread, but if you can't find them for your magical workings, do a quick search for a substitute—there's usually quite a list to choose from. No hard-and-fast rules apply when it comes to flower magic (as long as you're staying safe—not all flowers are friendly). Remember, it is what the flower says to you that is important. If you get a different vibe than I do from a flower, it doesn't mean you're wrong; it just means we're both individuals with our own unique mojo!

### Anise Hyssop (Agastache foeniculum)

I *will cheer you.*

This one always baffles me, because even though it's called anise hyssop, it's neither an anise nor a hyssop! It's a member of the mint (Lamiaceae) family. It's not native to my area, but it's a mint, which means we have no trouble naturalizing it in our yard. It has a lovely mauve flower and smells mildly of licorice.

The folklore of anise hyssop is interesting. When grown around the back door, it is said to be a protective herb. Magically it is used to assist with good communication, clear the air after an argument, or help alleviate feelings of guilt when the blame lies elsewhere or forgiveness has already been granted.

To make a sympathy sachet, I use a muslin bag to hold the herbs and a burlap bag for the outer covering. I place the dried anise hyssop leaves, as well as some sage, cedar, myrrh, and rosemary (all herbs that promote friendship, love, and understanding), into the muslin bag, and place that in the outer bag. Decorating the exterior is a wonderful chance to get creative. I've seen lovely hand-sewn quilted covers, and pouches that have been knitted or crocheted. The more energy that goes into it, the more successful the outcome will be.

Anise hyssop grows easily in USDA zones 5–10 and is a great pollinator in the garden. In addition to adding it to amulet bags, I also use it as a tea, because it is sweet-tasting and aids digestion. I include the dried leaves in protection incense blends and in bundles for people who have fallen out with each other and are seeking to reconcile.

### Beach Rose (Rosa Rugosa)

I *will teach you.*

My husband and I planted a *Rosa rugosa* hedge to the east of our little postage stamp of land, and have some growing in the orchard and alongside the front path, too. I make jam and wine with the hips—the name for the fruit of the rose. I use the thorns in protective magic. I've even made sorbet with the petals. Rose petals are where traditional Turkish delight candy gets its lovely pink color and light flavor.

Magically, the rose has myriad uses. It's related to both love and protection, so there's little surprise that it's often included in love potions and elixirs. Roses are also said to attract the fae folk. I use rose in my witch balls: the petals in love spells and the thorns in protection work. An electuary made from honey, cacao, and rose petals is not just delicious but has also been proven to be quite an aphrodisiac!

A very effective witch ball is easy and inexpensive to make. I use a clear glass Christmas tree ornament. Plastic will work, but I try to limit my use of plastic whenever possible (and I get a better vibe of energy from glass). For a protection witch ball, I add dried rose thorns, dried cloves, and a cinnamon stick. To fill the ball and make it look pretty, I include some floral moss, a bit of black-colored sand or gravel, and a scroll of intention written in black ink on a scrap of gray or red watercolor paper.

We grow beach roses because of their simplicity. *Rosa rugosa* has five petals; mine are magenta in color, and the perfume is very strong. They're fairly low-maintenance and recommended for USDA zones 3–9. They seem to like it here! I water them when it's too dry, feed them occasionally, and sometimes have to treat them with a homemade bug spray to keep the aphids off them. They're worth the little bit of management and attention that I do give them, and they respond well. They provide a protective thicket and a natural haven for wildlife, as well as valuable ingredients for my craft and the kitchen.

### Catmint (Nepeta mussinii)

I *will calm you.*

Catmint was one of the first herbs we planted when we moved here in 2006. It is a protective herb and a mild sedative and has lovely mauve-colored flowers in late summer. We don't have a cat—and yes, there is a difference between catnip (*Nepeta cataria*) and catmint (*Nepeta mussinii*). Catmint is a more compact plant with mauve flowers, while catnip is leggier and has white flowers. Magically the two are interchangeable.

When used in spells or rituals, catmint invites peace and contentment. When burned, it helps to repel unwanted insects, so it's particularly beneficial for outdoor ceremonies. Planted in the garden, catmint deters squash bugs and other pests. It's a love herb, but it's more the type of love that embraces compassion and understanding than romantic love.

I sometimes add catmint to my Call the Ancestors incense blend, particularly if I'm feeling a bit frazzled when seeking their counsel. A good recipe involves one part catmint, one part common sage, one part lavender, and one part cinnamon—all inexpensive and readily available. I put sand in the bottom of a heatproof dish, then break off a small piece of a charcoal briquette, light it, and carefully place it on the sand. I sprinkle the incense onto the glowing coal and focus on the matter in question. I find it handy to have pen and paper close so I can record my thoughts as they come to me in order to reflect on them later. Many a message has come to me via the smoke once I've taken the time to reflect on what the ramblings mean.

**I sometimes add catmint to my Call the Ancestors incense blend, particularly if I'm feeling a bit frazzled when seeking their counsel.... Many a message has come to me via the smoke once I've taken the time to reflect on what the ramblings mean.**

Catmint is easily obtained, but make sure it's catmint and not catnip. Catmint grows well in just about any soil and in USDA zones 4–8. With its spreading habit, it does have a tendency to take over, which we've found is useful for filling in areas between walkways. Catmint is considered to be lucky—and I'll take all the help I can get!

## Elder (Sambucus)

*I will inspire you.*

One of my favorite memories of living on the farm involves gathering elderberries one glorious late summer evening. My (then) husband and I had been loading up firewood; he was cutting it with the chain saw and I was chucking it into the trailer behind the tractor. There were a few pieces too large for me to handle, so while he was splitting them, I trundled off down the hill toward the canal and loaded up my hat with elderberries. They went into an elder and apple crumble for tea that evening, as the sun gave way to a star-filled night.

Elder needs to be respected—it's toxic unless cooked. However, when cooked, it's simply marvelous. The flowers and the berries can be used in many different recipes, mundane and magical. It's not surprising that qualities attributed to elder involve protection and abundance. Throughout history, elder has been treated with caution and respect; some thought it evil, and would never build houses or boats from its wood, believing that witches lived in it, and to bring it down would incur their wrath (Addison 1985, 90).

I'm a big believer in ingesting my magic whenever safe to do so, and the elder provides ample opportunities to do just this. Elderberry preserves, elderberry and apple pie, elderberry cordial, and elderberry wine are just some of the possibilities. Jam made in the summer from elderflowers, oranges, and a touch of cinnamon is not only delicious but will also help to ensure success. I gather the flowers in the morning when the dew is gone but before the sun becomes too hot. (It is also possible to use dried flowers for this, but remember that drying them will greatly decrease their volume, so be stingy—four elderflower tea bags should work.) I steep four cups of the freshly collected elderflowers with a small cinnamon stick in the same volume of water. To the strained liquid I add the juice and the zest of four large oranges and two cups of sugar. This is simmered gently until the liquid thickens, and when it has set, I put it in sterilized jars. It makes three half-pint jars of some of the most deliciously scented orange marmalade—just the thing for spreading on toast when I need to have a particularly productive day!

Elder is native to the US and grows in many soil conditions. It is hardy in USDA zones 3–8 and will grow to a substantial height and width. We have two different varieties of elder growing in our orchard: Johns and Adams. Cross-pollination is recommended. I will always have an elder somewhere on the property as long as it is possible.

### Thistle (*Cirsium vulgare*)

I *will protect you.*

My husband and I always have a playful debate when the thistles come up in the spring. He sees them as weeds, things that need to be pulled. I insist that they stay; they are gorgeous when blooming and the pollinators love them—and then I remind him that his father was from Aberdeen! (The thistle is the national flower of Scotland.)

Magically the thistle is a very protective herb. Anyone who has tried to dig one up knows that the roots go deep and the spines are sharp. Thistles lend those qualities to any spell or ritual. Planted around the house, they are wards of protection. When I was first drawn to thistle, I didn't find much information on it, so I set out to let the plant teach me. I learned that some plants want to be left alone; they would "bite" me when I tried to work with them. Others would let me take their flowers, spines, or seeds with ease. This led me to include thistle in work where standing one' s ground is important, where strong boundaries and persistence are necessary.

The dried spines of the thistle can be added to witch balls in the same way as rose thorns. In the past I have made protection amulets and poppets filled with dried thistle leaves. To make a protection shield sachet, you'll need dried thistle leaves or spines, some kapok fiber or other insulating fabric, and a small muslin bag or a square foot of cotton fabric and some twine. Put the thistles between two layers of the kapok, roll it up, then put it in a muslin bag (the kapok will stop the spines from poking through the fabric) or bundle it in the fabric square and tie it shut with the twine. Carry this with you when entering into an uncomfortable situation. I like to put a pinch of benzoin and a quartz crystal in with mine to amplify the energies. I stuff the poppets the same way.

Thistles are related to the gentle daisy. Supposedly thistles are edible, but I've never been tempted to eat one. We have an abundance of both pink and yellow thistles here, but I tend to favor the magenta ones. There are many species of both colors of thistles. For magical purposes, they are interchangeable—unless color magic is also involved.

### Yarrow (*Achillea millefolium*)

I *will encourage you to grow.*

I was given my starts of yarrow by another hedgewitch some time ago, and now it is well established in a large area of the yard. While commercially grown yarrow comes in a variety of colors, my husband and I are both very fond of the tall pinky-white flowers that appear on the meadow yarrow in late spring. It grows easily and spreads rapidly, which is helpful for filling in the area around the daylilies.

Magically yarrow has quite the history. Its name is said to come from a story about Achilles (Addison 1985, 316–17). I was always told to harvest its flowers on Midsummer's Day, when their energy is at their peak. A charm made from yarrow was said to ensure that love would last for at least seven years (Carr-Gomm 2008, 108–10). According to *Cunningham's Encyclopedia of Magical Herbs*, yarrow is an herb that brings courage and fidelity and increases psychic powers.

I add yarrow to my divination candles, and there are two ways of doing this. I use a soy-based wax, and—because I am a potter—I make the candle container myself, pressing yarrow leaves into the damp clay to create a pattern. (You do not have to go to this extreme; a store-bought candle in a glass jar will work just fine.) Once the pot is made and the candle has been poured, I decorate the surface of the wax with dried yarrow leaves and flowers, keeping them away from the wick so they melt into the wax as the candle is being burned. To do this with a jar candle, simply purchase one where the scent and the color reflect the desired outcome. Soften the top a bit with a hair dryer, then press the dried yarrow into the warm wax.

Yarrow is easy to grow. It is hardy in USDA zones 3–9 and spreads easily. It's great for attracting all kinds of pollinators, and its earthy smell often discourages bothersome bugs. Grown by the door, yarrow hinders unpleasant energies from entering. The dried flowers are attractive in autumn wreaths and other decor. All in all, I think yarrow is simply magical!

• • • • • • • • • • • • •

I've focused on my experiences with some of my favorite magical flowers in this article, but this list of garden companions is by no means comprehensive. I've shared what these plants mean to *me*, but it's your journey that's important. To explore your own relationship with herbs and flowers, grab your favorite gardening book or do a bit of online research. What flowers call to you? Which ones invite you on a magical journey? All journeys begin with one step. Where will the path of flower magic lead you?

## Resources

Addison, Josephine. *The Illustrated Plant Lore*. London: Sidgwick & Jackson, 1985.

Barker, Cicely Mary. *The Complete Book of the Flower Fairies*. London: Frederick Warne, 2002.

Carr-Gomm, Philip and Stephanie. *The Druid Plant Oracle*. New York: St. Martin's Press, 2008.

Cunningham, Scott. *Cunningham's Encyclopedia of Magical Herbs*. St. Paul, MN: Llewellyn, 1985.

Davies, Jill. *A Garden of Miracles*. New York: Beaufort Books, 1985.

Rose, Jeanne. *Herbs & Things: Jeanne Rose's Herbal*. New York: Perigee Trade, 1973.

Rudginsky, Marlene. *The Flower Speaks*. Stamford, CT: US Games Systems, 1999.

Tierra, Michael. *Herbal Tarot*. Stamford, CT: U.S. Games Systems, 1999.

**Charlie Rainbow Wolf** *is happiest when she is creating something, especially if it can be made from items that others have cast aside. An artist, author, alchemist, and astrologer, Charlie immerses herself deep into the roots of living, but she happily confesses she's easily distracted because life offers so many wonderful things to explore. She follows an herbal mystery path, is an advocate of organic gardening and cooking, and in her downtime relaxes with a bit of knitting. She lives in the Midwest with her husband and special-needs Great Danes. Visit www.charlierainbow.com.*

**Illustrator: Tim Foley**

# Personal Correspondence: Adapting Traditional Tables of Correspondence

*Emily Carlin*

A witch's choices, from what color of candles to burn to which herbs to put in our tea, are guided by what energies we want to bring into our lives. Every object in the world has a unique energetic resonance. To find out what magickal intention that resonance corresponds with, we often look to published tables of correspondence. These tables reflect the common consensus of what things correspond to within a particular tradition or practice. While they're fantastic resources, these tables are only the beginning. To take your practice to the next level, you must adapt and augment traditional tables of correspondence to account for your location and personal experiences.

## Localization

One of the stumbling blocks to effectively using published correspondences is that they cannot take into account the many different environments in which practitioners live today. It's hardly surprising that the original creators of these tables generally chose to include the plants, stones, directions, and so on, that were common to their local areas. Unfortunately, since many of those original creators were concentrated in specific geographic areas, not all of the natural items commonly listed are readily available or particularly relevant to practitioners in the rest of the world.

This disconnect is most clearly seen when it comes to plants. For example, Buckram (*Allium ursinum*) is a type of wild garlic that is fairly common in English forests but is rarely found elsewhere. Finding such an herb in a table of correspondence wouldn't be particularly useful to practitioners outside of England unless they were enthusiastic gardeners. Similarly, the common magickal herb damiana (*Turnera diffusa*) is native to Central America and the Caribbean and doesn't grow well outside a subtropical climate. Practitioners wishing to use damiana almost always have to order dried plants from hundreds, if not thousands, of miles away. While commercially purchased dried plants from far-flung locations can be used to good effect in magick, it's not always the best option.

The two main reasons that local ingredients are often preferred in magick are expense and energy. Apart from the obvious purchase price, ingredients from across the globe have costs in labor, packing, shipping, carbon emissions, and storage. Unless the growers are known

and trusted, a practitioner can't be sure of the energies imparted to the ingredients during planting, growing, and harvesting. The energies of exploited land and undervalued labor are hardly conducive to effective magick. Better to use local ingredients where you know what you're getting.

Further, ingredients that come from the same area where you practice will usually have stronger energies and integrate more easily into your spellwork. Natural ingredients will always have the strongest energies when they are alive and in their native environment. While harvested and dried herbs can remain magickally viable for over a year when stored properly, they will never have the same potency as something freshly picked.

Locally produced ingredients will also already incorporate local energies and thus have an easier time resonating with the energies of a local practitioner. This synergy can be enhanced when a practitioner takes the time to know local plants and develop an energetic relationship with them. (There are whole volumes of work on plant communication and plant spirit medicine that can be researched.) The energetic potency of a plant that's been sustainably harvested, with permission, by a practitioner who has a relationship with said plant will always be stronger and easier to work with than something that's been sitting on a shelf for who knows how long.

There are many ways to determine the correspondences for local plants, including looking to indigenous beliefs, divination, plant spirit communication, and intuition. The indigenous mythology of your area is likely to include magickal properties for local plants, trees, rocks, etc. When done mindfully and with respect for their cultural context, these correspondences can often be used by non-indigenous practitioners. However, if not done respectfully, this practice can lead to cultural appropriation, so use good judgment.

Divination is a simple, and less potentially problematic, method for finding local correspondences. Pendulums and dowsing tools are particularly helpful. To find a plant or stone with the correspondence desired, simply go outside and ask the tool to lead you to an object willing to aid you. When a suitable object is found, ask the divination tool to confirm that you've found the right thing. Of course, if you are able to communicate with plant spirits, then you can commune with particular plants, befriend them, and ask them their correspondences. This type of communication and relationship-building takes a fair amount of skill and effort, but the energetic bonds that result make the plant's willing offerings especially useful in spellwork. Even if you are not able to directly communicate with plant spirits, you may feel an intuitive pull to use a particular plant for a particular purpose. Trust that intuition and, if you feel the need, validate your intuition with divination. Any of these methods can help you determine a set of working correspondences for the flora and fauna native to your environment. Choose whichever method fits best with your practice and experiment to determine what feels best for you.

## Personal Resonance

Another weakness of traditional tables of correspondence is that they cannot take a practitioner's personal experiences into account. A practitioner's ability to unify the energies of their intent with the spell components they have chosen is critical for a successful working. That means a practitioner has to believe in the correspondences they use deeply enough to connect with them energetically; the more strongly the practitioner believes, the easier it will be to connect and thus the more powerful the magick.

Unfortunately, traditional correspondences don't necessarily resonate with everyone. A spell for friendship using traditional correspondences may involve a pink candle dressed with juniper oil for healthy affection and a jade figurine of a dog for loyal friendship. While this would work for many, what if the practitioner had a bad experience with dogs or is allergic to juniper? Said practitioner would have to either fight to align their energies to that of the published correspondences or return to their tables and look for possible substitutes. What about a practitioner who doesn't feel any resonance at all with what's in the books? The answer, of course, is to develop their own set of correspondences.

Throughout our lives, all of us develop vast reservoirs of personal experiences. These experiences create meaning and symbolism that are unique to each of us. These personal symbols naturally resonate with us far more deeply than anything picked out of a book. If a practitioner were given a dandelion on their first date and on every subsequent anniversary with the love of their life, a dandelion would be a more potent symbol for love in their workings than any red rose. This personal resonance extends beyond singular objects to places with potent emotional history, sense memories, and even quotes from favorite books or movies.

**Throughout our lives, all of us develop vast reservoirs of personal experiences. These experiences create meaning and symbolism that are unique to each of us. These personal symbols naturally resonate with us far more deeply than anything picked out of a book.**

To begin identifying personal symbols, reflect on the things that have carried meaning throughout your life. It's easiest to start by identifying life's big events and the things you associate with them. Think of your school colors, the flowers at your best friend's wedding, the flavors of a meal celebrating the start of a new career, or the smell of your favorite summer camp. Think about the things you run into that suddenly evoke powerful memories, like the song that sends you back to a high school dance, the smell that takes you back to your grandmother's kitchen, or the book you reread to be ten years old again. These are the things that can be used as potent magickal symbols. The power of your memories and associations preload these things with energy while in your hands.

Family traditions are another rich source of personal symbolism. For example, I had my tonsils removed when I was six years old, and my father gave me a stuffed purple dragon as a get well gift. The next time a family member had a hospital visit, the stuffed dragon was passed on to them as a get well gift, and they in turn passed on the dragon to the next relative who needed it. This tradition still continues today, with the stuffed dragon having passed hands over a dozen times. While a purple cartoon dragon isn't going to be found on any table of correspondence associated with healing, there is no better symbol for those in my family. Keep in mind that "family" is not limited to family of blood. Our families of choice, be they friends, coworkers, or community members, also have traditions and associations that can be drawn upon in magick.

Not all personal symbols and associations are so obvious. For many people, the things that mean the most to them are normal, ubiquitous things. Simple things like your favorite comfort food, songs you love, the scent of your mom's shampoo, quotes from your favorite books or movies, memes, and even video games can immediately trigger a particular energy or emotion. For example, a sonic cleansing done with a favorite pop song can be just as effective as one performed with a tuning fork or bell, depending on which one means more to the practitioner. These everyday things make wonderful magickal components with intrinsic meaning and potency for your practice.

By exploring memories and associations, we can find powerful correspondences that elevate our spellwork. Using these personal correspondences, a practitioner might return to the previous example of a friendship spell and make it their own by using a candle that's the same blue as the house of their childhood best friend, dressed with oregano-infused olive oil that reminds them of spaghetti dinners with college friends, and two action figures of Steve Rogers and Bucky Barnes—the inseparable best friends of the practitioner's favorite movies and comic books. Tradition wouldn't intrinsically attribute friendship to any of these things, but the deep meaning they have for the practitioner makes them the perfect spell components. The deep emotional connection that a practitioner has with personal correspondences adds power and energetic fluidity to spellwork.

## Creating Your Own Tables of Correspondence

After exploring the potential of local ingredients and personal resonances, you can create tables of correspondence that are solely your own. Begin by listing the magickal intentions for which correspondences are needed. Common categories include health, wealth, success, love, luck, justice, communication, cleansing, protection, banishing, and psychic power. Also take some time to reflect on any less common or nontraditional intentions you might wish to add to your tables. For example, an attorney might add persuasion or insight and a software developer might add coding skills or project management. After your categories are listed, go through your findings of local and personal correspondences and organize them into your table. You now have a personalized table of correspondence that lists objects and symbols that have strong resonance for you, for all the types of spellwork you commonly perform.

Personal tables of correspondence are highly dynamic. As life moves forward and people evolve and change, so too do the things that hold meaning for them. As we have new experiences, new things will gain meaning for us and older associations may fade and be replaced. This means you should periodically update your personal correspondences to ensure you're using associations that still hold meaning for you. Doing so annually, at Samhain or a milestone with personal associations of growth and renewal, will ensure up-to-date and potent personal correspondences.

## Using Personal Correspondences

While personal correspondences are a wonderful tool much of the time, they are not always appropriate. Use them freely when crafting new workings. Spells you craft for personal use will always benefit from correspondences that hold special meaning for you. Use them more cautiously when adapting older workings to changed environments and situations, particularly if the original working is from a specific culture or tradition. Preexisting spells must always be evaluated in the context for which they were created before any substitutions are made. Do the spell components have cultural weight beyond their obvious correspondences? Are there devotional requirements that prohibit substitutions? Would the spell lose meaning, and therefore potency, if substitutions were made? Many traditions make use of the power of repetition, doing things the same way over time to increase a practitioner's fluency and ease the

**Spells you craft for personal use will always benefit from correspondences that hold special meaning for you. Use them more cautiously when adapting older workings to changed environments and situations.**

movement of energy. Altering such workings could diminish their potency or remove vital cultural context. In such instances, you would be better off creating an entirely new working than altering the original. By balancing the innovation and creativity made possible through personal correspondences with respect for the power of tradition, you can have the best of both worlds.

You can greatly enhance your use of correspondences through localization and exploration of personal resonance. Using spell components native to your environment maximizes their potency and boosts their effectiveness. Working with items and symbols that have personal meaning also intensifies their power. To then mindfully incorporate these robust correspondences into your spellwork allows you to maximize the creativity and strength of your workings without extra energetic cost. Take your spellwork to the next level and create something uniquely your own with personal correspondences.

**Emily Carlin** *is a Witch, writer, teacher, and mediator based in Seattle. She currently teaches one-on-one online and at in-person events on the West Coast. During her twenty-plus years of practice, she has published articles on defensive magick, pop-culture magick, Santa Muerte, general Witchcraft, and more. For more information, visit http://www.e-carlin.com.*

**Illustrator: Bri Hermanson**

# Lights, Camera, Magick! Films That Belong in Your Witchy Library

*Najah Lightfoot*

In the 2011 movie *Hugo*, an orphaned boy lives in a clock tower, desperately searching for the key that will unlock the magic his father left behind. Through his search we enter the realm of cinematography in its earliest beginnings. We become aware of the ability of films to take us to places that exist only in our imagination, and we come to appreciate the childlike wonder and awe that lives within all of us.

As Witches, one of our greatest assets is our ability to visualize and use our imagination. It is no wonder then that many of us are film buffs, and when we find worlds that we dream of or see our visions portrayed in cinema, we become so attached to that film that it actually becomes part of our magickal experience.

That's what happens to me when I watch movies. I meld with them. They become touchstones, portals, gateways where I can leave the mundane world behind and enter into that space I believe in so strongly, with my witchy mind, body, and spirit. Perhaps you feel the same way or experience movies similarly. For these reasons, I have chosen seven films, out of countless reels, that I feel belong in every Witch's film library.

Not all the films presented here resonate with the topic "Witch," but what they do share is that deep, eerie, magickal, transcendent nature of the occult. They are films that are sure to make an impression on your consciousness as well as your subconscious witchy self. They are films that will stay with you long after the credits have rolled; films that you may return to time after time because you've found ideas or inspiration within them to help you carry on in your Witch life.

Space is limited, so I cannot list *all* the films I love or feel belong in your witchy film library. I've included movies that have made an impression on my witchy mind, and every time I watch them, I get something new from them. I've also added a couple of my favorites that may not be on everyone's radar.

So light your candles and grab some popcorn and your favorite libation. It's time for lights, camera, magick!

## Mary Poppins (1964)

My first magickal movie experience was the original *Mary Poppins*. I was captivated by the notion that one could jump through pictures drawn in chalk on a sidewalk, and that a tuppence could feed pigeons if you gave it to an old woman sitting on the steps of St. Paul's Cathedral in London. So affected was I that fifty years after I first saw the film, I stood before St. Paul's Cathedral upon those very steps! It took me decades to make it to London, but make it I did. Never give up on your childhood dreams and fantasies!

## Willy Wonka and the Chocolate Factory (1971)

The second magickal film that has held great influence over my life is the original *Willy Wonka and the Chocolate Factory* starring Gene Wilder. Are you kidding? Who doesn't want a golden ticket? And wouldn't you know it, decades later, after appearing at a bookstore launch and signing for my book *Good Juju: Mojos, Rites & Practices for the Magical Soul*, I received a golden bookmark!

Movies can and do influence our minds, dreams, goals, and aspirations. They show us what is possible if only we believe. They also show us what bad things might happen if we insist on moving in a certain direction, and they bring to life the monsters we all know are there, leaving us frightened to go to sleep—but then seeking magickal ways to combat them. They show us that different dimensions exist, and yes indeed we can travel to them, and sometimes through movies we can go back into the past and visit worlds we wished we had lived in. Let us delve into the magical lands of cinema and see where the dial of time, space, belief, and the power of Witchcraft takes us!

## Angel Heart (1987)

This movie captures the noir of New Orleans and our fascination with the occult and Conjure. I like to say that "it put somethin' on me." I've never forgotten this film's eerie, haunting theme and disturbing imagery, yet I've been drawn to watch it more than once. Perhaps you will too.

## The Ninth Gate (1999)

What Witch doesn't love rare, old books? Books found in antiquarian bookstores filled with occult symbols, woodcuts, and puzzling tarot images? It's even better if that book will lead you to the Wizard or Witch you seek to further your path into the Mysteries. This film hits all those points. It's a good one for looking at how the occult can be a vehicle to places one might think twice about visiting.

## The Skeleton Key (2005)

This movie is filled with haunting images and a story line that will make you believe in the power of red brick dust, ghosts, and spirits. It features the wonderful countryside of Louisiana as well as some brief stops in the Crescent City of New Orleans. It reminds us that magick lives right alongside us in our everyday lives, whether we choose to believe in it or not.

## To Sleep with Anger (1990)

In this film, a man loses his "toby" and an uninvited guest comes to visit. When you've got the blues for Hoodoo and country folk trying to live city ways, light a candle and watch this film. Two big brown thumbs-up for the almost 100 percent Black cast, including an actor you might recognize from their role in *Eve's Bayou.*

## Willow (1988)

In this movie, the incomparable pioneers of film Ron Howard and George Lucas created a world featuring adventure and magical questing. One of the things I love most about the character of Willow is that he is a person of small stature and lives in a village full of diversity. It's quite a treat to see a "medieval" village filled with such different and engaging characters! This may be an older film, but its place in cinematic history has been secured. You can also watch it with your kids, which is a nice thing to do. Not all witchy and occult-based films need to be scary and full of disturbing or gory images. (Well, there is one icky scene in this one.) Plus, if you're a Val Kilmer fan, it's great to see him in all his glory playing the role of Madmartigan in this movie.

**Najah Lightfoot** *is the multi-award-winning author of the best-selling* Good Juju: Mojos, Rites & Practices for the Magical Soul. *She is a regular contributor to the Llewellyn annuals and a contributor to* The Library of Esoterica, Volume III: Witchcraft. *Her magickal staff is part of the permanent collection at the* Buckland Museum of Witchcraft & Magick, *located in Cleveland, Ohio. Najah is a fellow of the Sojourner Truth Leadership Circle, sponsored by Auburn Seminary, and an initiate of a private* New Orleans Vodou Society. *She lives in Denver, Colorado, where the blue skies and the power of the Rocky Mountains uplift and fill her soul. She can be found online at www.twitter.com/NajahLightfoot, www.facebook.com/NajahLightfoot, and www.instagram.com/NajahLightfoot.*

**Illustrator: Bri Hermanson**

# The Witch's Book of Shadows: Create Your Own Book of Knowledge and Wisdom

*Deborah Blake*

Witches use all kinds of tools to help them practice their craft, from athames to wands and everything in between. Some of these tools help us to direct energy, others serve the function of increasing the force of a spell, and others hone our focus so that our magical work might be as powerful as possible. Tools can range from the basic, like a simple white candle, to the ornate, like a carved and bejeweled goblet. What is really important is that they are useful or beautiful, or both, and that they feed our witchy spirits.

This is definitely something that can be said of a Book of Shadows.

A Book of Shadows is the term for a book in which a Witch keeps their accumulated magical knowledge, and to which they add any additional information garnered throughout the years of their Witchcraft practice. This particular name probably originated with Gerald Gardner in the 1940s, but there have been magical books, often called grimoires, throughout history, in cultures as varied as the Greeks, the ancient Jews, and the Gnostic sects of Christianity.

So what is the purpose of a Book of Shadows, how do you create one, and how do you use it once you have one? And what do you do if you want a Book of Shadows but don't feel up to the task of starting one from scratch? Not to worry—I have the answers to all those questions.

## Why Use a Book of Shadows?

It has been said that all you need to practice Witchcraft is mind, heart, and spirit, but a certain amount of knowledge can be helpful, too. We all start out at the beginning knowing little more than that we are attracted to nature, and perhaps the concept of a goddess in addition to a god, and more than likely we are intrigued by the spark that is magic. From there, all our paths are different, but each one of us learns as we go, gathering information about both the concepts behind Witchcraft and the practical aspects of how to integrate it into our lives.

For many of us, that means learning from other Witches in person or from books, plus, of course, our own experiences as we cast spells, perform rituals, and create charm bags or poppets or talismans. For a long time I had binders filled with sheets I'd copied, and most of my Witchcraft books (and we're talking a *lot* of books here—shelves and shelves of books) had so many skinny sticky notes and bookmarks that they looked like some form of deranged porcupine.

What I needed was a place to gather the information I used most often in one place, where it would be easily accessible when I needed to find a spell or look up the correspondences most appropriate for magical work toward a specific goal. And that's where a Book of Shadows comes in. It is your own personal reference source, if that's how you choose to use it, as well as an ongoing record of the magical work you've done.

## Creating a Book of Shadows

The first thing you need to do is figure out what kind of Book of Shadows you want. Simple or involved? Will you want to write in it by hand (in which case you might prefer lined paper) or tape in information you've printed out (in which case blank pages might be best)? Do you expect to use it for a long time? Then you might want to get a larger book.

Once you have some idea of how you will be using your Book of Shadows, you can start by making or buying a blank book to use. There are lots of wonderful premade blank books intended for witchy use, with moons or pentacles or other magical symbols on the cover. But you can also take a plain notebook or binder and decorate it yourself. If you are really crafty, you can make the entire book, using heavy paper like poster board for the outside and something more light-weight on the inside. Punch holes in the edges and lace ribbon or yarn through the holes to make a book. Then you can add pages whenever you want.

Finding or making the book itself is just the first step. Then you have to figure out what you want to include between the covers.

My group, Blue Moon Circle, has a Book of Shadows that we started with our first meeting way back in 2004. At the front it holds the names of those who have been members, including the three founding Witches who are still a part of it to this day, as well as a prayer/spell for its positive use and a copy of the Charge of the Goddess. Since then we've also added all the spells and rituals we've done as a group, and even pictures of our time together, both in and out of circle.

This is probably the simplest example of a Book of Shadows—merely a record of spells and rituals, with a few small personal additions that mean something to the person or people the Book belongs to.

On the other end of the spectrum is a much more inclusive book, which might contain those things but also information about all the components that go into magical work, as well as journal entries about dreams, tarot readings, and the like, and even recipes for feasts. There is really no limit to what you can put in your Book of Shadows—it is completely up to you.

Here is a list of things you might include in your Book of Shadows:

- Herbs
- Stones and crystals
- Candles (color correspondences, decorating tips, etc.)
- Magical recipes for oils, charm bags, poppets, and more
- Divination practice you have done for yourself or readings from others
- Gods and goddesses
- The elements
- Invocations and quarter calls
- Spells (and whether or not they were successful)
- Rituals (both ones you put on for yourself and those you attend)
- Recipes for feasts, cakes and ale, and kitchen witchery
- Lists of correspondences for magical work
- Photos or sketches of altars you've set up, events you've attended, full moons, and more

Depending on what you want to include, you will then need to decide how you are going to organize your Book of Shadows, if in fact you are going to organize it at all. Blue Moon Circle just went chronologically: each ritual we did together was entered into the book after we did it, so it starts with our first gathering in 2004 and continues to the present day.

If you are planning to have a Book of Shadows with information on herbs, stones, and other things, you may want to set it up divided into sections that you can add to as you go along, so you aren't flipping through the entire book every time you are looking for which crystal is associated with love.

## How to Use a Book of Shadows

Whether you have made your own Book of Shadows or are using one created by someone else, like my book *The Eclectic Witch's Book of Shadows: Witchy Wisdom at Your Fingertips*, the answer to the question of how to use your book is pretty much the same—any way you want to.

Some people use a Book of Shadows purely as a reference. It is where they store their magical knowledge and where they look when they need to know a specific fact or find the spell they did the last time they were going on a long trip. It is basically their own personal encyclopedia of Witchcraft.

Others use their book more like a journal, making notes about anything and everything that has an impact on their spiritual life. They may write down dreams that seem particularly meaningful or signs that appear to them that might be messages from the gods, or they might pull a tarot card every day and write down how the day turned out.

You can write things in your book by hand, but don't be intimidated if your handwriting isn't very good. (Mine is atrocious, and it would take me hours to write neatly enough that I could read it again later, so I tend to type up my information and print it out in a nice font instead.) If you are the only one using the book, it doesn't matter if it is a little sloppy.

Many people also add little drawings or sketches to their entries, like flowers or herbs, or symbols that showed up in dreams or divination. *The Eclectic Witch's Book of Shadows* has a lot of wonderful illustrations in it already, but there is still room for you to add your own.

In fact, if you are using my book, there are also many places for you to add your own notes. You can supplement the herbs, stones, and deities listed in the book with others you particularly connect with, or make notations about which ones seem to work the best for you.

Whether you are using a book you made from scratch, one you adapted to be a Book of Shadows, or a book like mine that was created by someone else, there are a few steps you can take to make it truly your own (or your coven's, if you are sharing a Book of Shadows within a group). Here are a few suggestions:

1. **Write your name in the book.** This may seem like a no-brainer, but names have power, and writing your name (either your formal name or your magical name, if you have one) inside the front cover shows that you claim the magic within as your own. You can simply use your signature, or you can print out "This book belongs to _____." If you have a symbol that has meaning to you (I use a cat stamp, for instance, and one of my covenmates signs her name with a bat outline underneath it), you can add that too.

2. **Bless and consecrate the book.** Many Witches bless and consecrate all their new tools, and you can certainly do this with your Book of Shadows as well. There are many different approaches to doing this, but I like to call on the elements and the Goddess to bless the book using salt and water (earth and water), a stick of burnable purifying herbs or incense (air), and

a candle (fire). Place the Book of Shadows on an altar or a piece of cloth. Sprinkle it with salt and say, "I bless this book with the power of earth." Sprinkle a little water over the book with your fingertips, being careful not to damage the surface, and say, "I bless this book with the power of water." Light your stick of purifying herbs or incense and wave it over the book and say, "I bless this book with the power of air." Then light a candle (white is good, or yellow for mind and intellect) and say, "I bless this book with the power of fire." You can either light an additional candle to stand for the Goddess and/or God or simply hold the book up toward the sky and say, "I bless and consecrate this book in the name of the God and Goddess, for positive magical work. So mote it be." (If you follow a particular deity, you can substitute their name.)

3. **Write something in the book.** It doesn't matter what. It can be a favorite spell, your magical goals, or even a prayer—whatever feels right to you in that moment.

A Witch's tools are important to their practice, and having your own personal Book of Shadows gives you one more tool to use as you walk your path toward being the best possible Witch—and human being—you can be. May you use it well.

**Deborah Blake** *is the author of over a dozen books on modern Witchcraft, including* The Little Book of Cat Magic *and* Everyday Witchcraft, *as well as the acclaimed* Everyday Witch Tarot *and* Everyday Witch Oracle *decks. She has also written three paranormal romance and urban fantasy series for Berkley, and her new cozy mystery series launched with* Furbidden Fatality *in 2021. Deborah lives in a 130-year-old farmhouse in upstate New York with numerous cats who supervise all her activities, both magical and mundane. She can be found at http://deborahblakeauthor.com.*

**Illustrator: M. Kathryn Thompson**

# The Power of Plants: Using Herbs in Your Magick

A.C. *Fisher Aldag*

Witches have long been portrayed as using herbs to make potions or healing brews and doing spellwork involving magickal plants. In this article I'll focus on finding plant "allies," or helpers, preserving herbs, and the essentials of using plants in rituals and workings. All you really need for herbal magick are the proverbial root, leaf, and branch, a few cooking tools, water, a stovetop, a couple of books on herbalism, and your own personal enchantment.

My family and I have been gardening, homesteading, and gathering plants for around twenty-five years, and I've been

practicing the *artes magickal* for over forty years. I've done lots of experimentation and made dozens of mistakes along the way, but here are some tried-and-true tools and methods of using herbs for magick that I've discovered.

## Intent

First, you might want to think about what you intend for your magickal working to accomplish. If you have a specific spell in mind, read the list of ingredients or look up correspondences that relate to your desired condition. A good herbal book will give suggestions about which plants symbolize what situation. For example, the common dandelion represents strength, the male principle, solar energies, and resilience. Herbals also give suggestions about the best times to work with plants according to the moon phase, the day of the week, and the signs of the zodiac. For instance, if you need vitality, gather nettles when the sun is in Leo. If you desire love and purity, pick apple blossoms on a Friday during the night just after the springtime new moon. You will also wish to consider if the plants you're planning to use are for ingesting, topical application (like a lotion or ointment), or simply to attract a certain entity or condition—for instance, as a bouquet on your altar or in a potion within a cauldron.

If you seek healing, an herbal can also tell you what plant can be beneficial in treating any given ailment. Astringent witch hazel is wonderful for skin conditions, but you'd not want to drink it to soothe an upset stomach. Mint tea is better for helping calm a bellyache. All of this may sound daunting at first, but herbals can tell you what you need to know. Resources such as Scott Cunningham's *Encyclopedia of Magical Herbs*, Llewellyn's yearly *Herbal Almanacs*, and/or *The Herb Gardener's Essential Guide* by Sandra Kynes impart some amazing esoteric uses for plants.

## Sources

Foraging for plants provides a unique experience to interact with the sacred Earth. However, you can obtain everything you need at metaphysical shops, health food stores, or online apothecaries. You might want to purchase a few herbs that cover the basics: basil, cilantro, cinnamon, cloves, oregano, parsley, pepper, rosemary, sage, and thyme for culinary purposes; catnip, chamomile, lemongrass, mint, and raspberry leaf for soothing teas; and aloe, goldenseal root, motherwort, and yarrow for assistance in healing. All of these plants have a magickal component as well. Check your own yard before you buy—you could likely find dandelions, chicory, plantain, Queen Anne's lace, and violets growing within feet of your door.

Some products may carry a label that tells you if the plant was harvested and preserved according to an appropriate astrological event. You'll want your allies to be ethically sourced as well. Before hitting your local store or herbalist, read up on which plants are becoming threatened. Trees such as palo santo of Central and South America and sandalwood of Southwest Asia are becoming scarce in their native homes. It's usually easy to replace an ingredient in a potion with something less scarce.

## Tools and Methods

Some esoteric traditions use tools such as a white-handled athame (knife) or a bronze boline (sickle) for harvesting herbs. From a practical standpoint, a kitchen knife or scissors will work just as well, but a special bespelled blade can add extra magickal potency. Voice your intent as you cut your herbs (or as you buy them from an esoteric shop), for example, "This mugwort will bring me lucid dreams." If you don't know what you're going to use the plant for, a general blessing will do, like "This lavender will bring me joy."

The stereotypical media witch is often portrayed brewing a mysterious mixture in an iron cauldron over an open fire. However, iron is not always best for creating herbal concoctions, nor is copper or aluminum, as these metals can release ions into hot water or a heated ointment, which can alter the chemical composition of a plant. Iron can also nullify the magickal essence of herbs. Kitchen witches often use stainless steel pans, granite-coated pots, or glass or ceramic vessels for their workings. Your coven cauldron is fine to use if you're concocting a nondigestible potion.

**Iron can also nullify the magickal essence of herbs. Kitchen witches often use stainless steel pans, granite-coated pots, or glass or ceramic vessels for their workings. Your coven cauldron is fine to use if you're concocting a nondigestible potion.**

Wooden, granite-coated, stainless steel, or even plastic spoons are best for the same reason: they don't contaminate the herb during cooking. Stirring a mixture clockwise (deosil, sunwise) can help in invoking or summoning a desired condition, while stirring anticlockwise (widdershins, wraingates) can promote banishing or removing a certain situation.

A mortar and pestle can be helpful for grinding dried plant materials. Grind clockwise for creating and counterclockwise for dismissing. A good strainer is essential, and cheesecloth or muslin fabric is also useful to strain leaves out of brews or ointments. Get a few different sizes, from a big colander to small tea strainers. Dark-colored jars help to prevent sunlight from spoiling the herbal elixir, or store your concoctions in a cool, dark cabinet.

There is a debate about rehydrating or cooking plants used for spellwork. Some witches prefer not to use a microwave oven out of concern that the rays can interfere with the plant's natural oils or energetic properties. I prefer to brew my herbal mixtures on my old-fashioned wood-burning cookstove, although electric or gas ranges work just as well.

## Fun with Foraging

Hunting for herbs can add ambience. It's an opportunity to get out into nature, observe some birds and wild animals, and reconnect with the earth. But first, some words of caution: Before you begin harvesting wild and semi-domestic plants for food and herbal medicine, get a good field guide with photos so you can identify the species and learn which of the weeds can be toxic. Or look online, where there are many fine resources. Start by searching for "poisonous plants in my state." Be sure you can tell the difference between plants with a similar appearance. Water hemlock, which resembles a tall Queen Anne's lace or wild parsley, is deadly.

If you seek traditional witches' herbs that are named in some spells, use caution, as some of these, called "bane plants," are toxic or even poisonous. American aconite, although different from the European species called monkshood, still can be dangerous. Black nightshade, with its white pentagram-shaped flowers and black berries, and bittersweet nightshade, which has purple star blossoms and red berries, can grow in gardens between tomatoes, eggplants, and peppers, to whom they are vaguely related. The flowers, leaves, and berries are toxic, especially to children and pets. Jimsonweed/thorn apple/datura is prickly, causes an itchy sting if touched, and can be poisonous or even deadly if ingested. If you're planning to harvest potentially harmful herbs like nightshade or datura, wear gloves to avoid getting their alkaloid sap on your skin, and place them in containers that are well labeled. Learn everything about these plants before gathering them, and especially before using them. Handle with care.

Get a pamphlet from your local university, botanist, or county extension office to identify beneficial mushrooms and fungi, such as chicken of the woods, morels, and puffballs. Unless you are an expert, leave the toadstools alone.

Check to make sure that the plants you are picking have not been sprayed with a pesticide. Wash everything and pat it dry before using.

Also ensure that you're obeying the law. Gathering plants is forbidden in some protected parks and wild areas, while most roadside meadows and ditches are fair game. Be sure to leave a few wildflowers to propagate—don't be "that person" who picks the very last purple coneflower. Know which plants are endangered, such as wild trilliums, and take a picture to use in your working rather than plucking the plant itself.

Many practitioners prefer to harvest herbs on a particular sabbat, such as Midsummer/Alban Hefin/Litha for cutting St. John's wort and picking strawberries, or Lammas/Lughnasadh/Calan Awst for chopping down grains and hunting wild bilberries or blueberries. Some plants are best obtained during a certain moon phase, like American mandrake/mayapple during the full moon. Timing can heighten the effectiveness of a magickal working, so consider consulting a calendar or datebook to learn the astrological signs and moon phases.

When you do pick a plant in the wild, it's considered proper to leave an offering, such as a seashell, a pretty rock, or a poem or song. Expressions of thanks are also appreciated.

## How to Preserve Magickal Plants

For esoteric rites as well as cooking, fresh is best, as newly picked herbs contain more of the plant's natural oils. However, if they're to be placed into a talisman or saved to use later, plants must be dried or preserved to prevent rot. Hang them upside down to dry, head or top facing the floor, covered by a paper bag or muslin cloth to prevent contamination by dust and bugs as well as loss of seeds or leaves. Alternatively, cover the plants with paper towels or cheesecloth and leave them to dry on a countertop, turning them over daily until fully dry, or else put them in a food dryer.

If you intend to use plants for tea or a sachet, you might want to strip the dried leaves from the stems. The leaves are mostly used for simples and cooking, while the stems can be ground into a powder with a mortar and pestle. Powders do not work very well in teas but are good for incense, washes, and ointments. Stems can also be burned for smoke-cleansing. Roots are often boiled to release their natural oils, or chopped or ground and dried. In spells, roots can also be used whole. Some practitioners use a root as an alraun or poppet, carving a face into it and dressing it in tiny clothes, and even adding hair for effect.

**If you intend to use plants for tea or a sachet, you might want to strip the dried leaves from the stems. The leaves are mostly used for simples and cooking, while the stems can be ground into a powder with a mortar and pestle.**

Dried plants and plants mixed with alcohol or oils can be stored in glass bottles, canning jars, or even plastic in a cool, dark place such as a cupboard. Label them so you don't have to guess which is peppermint for tea, chocolate mint for baking, or pennyroyal for deterring insects and baneful entities. Brews and teas should be refrigerated and are only good for a few days.

## Herbs for Healing

Many plants can be ingested for their healing properties. Echinacea/purple coneflower, in capsule form or infused into a tea, helps to boost natural immunity. Do not use an aluminum tea ball, as the metal can cause a chemical reaction with the oils in the plants. Some herbs can be used topically, on the skin, as well as internally. For example, goldenseal root powder has astringent properties and can function as a natural antibiotic and detoxifier. Other plants are for topical use only, such as geranium, tansy, eucalyptus, and pennyroyal. The plant's leaves are infused in water, which can then be sprayed onto the skin to repel insects.

Dandelion, cleavers, itchweed/stinging nettle, burdock, yellow dock, and thistle grow in lawns and meadowlands, and while they can be annoying to homeowners, they all have medicinal properties. These allies can be infused into a tea as a spring tonic, said to restore vitality. Any plant with hairy leaves should be thoroughly strained from a liquid before using. Motherwort, red clover, and red raspberry leaves are useful for the issues associated with menstruation. White willow bark's interior layer helps ease a headache. Slippery elm, horehound, and cherry bark help quiet a cough. Eucalyptus hung from the showerhead can release its healing essences into the steam. Plantain is good for practically everything, including healing tonics and poultices for wounds or strained muscles. Trefoil and cinquefoil have no particular curative properties, but their three and five leaves, respectively, are sacred numbers that give any mixture a magickal boost. Foxglove, or the fairy cap, is used in medical digitalis, which can regulate heart rhythms but should be researched and used with great caution. Jewelweed, with its golden flowers and squishy leaves, grows well in ditches or swampland and is great for applying to insect stings. Milkweed sap can help to reduce a wart. Mullein leaves, dampened and applied whole, soothe skin conditions.

## Plants for Magick

Mullein flower spikes can be dried and burned as a witches' candle, especially on Midsummer night. Wild blackberry canes can be burned for smoke cleansing, as can a bundle of cedar, sweetgrass, and/or sage. White clover has long been a symbol of good luck. Sunflowers summon solar energies and good cheer. Wild rose flowers attract love. Thistle is a symbol of protection. Wormwood can expel negative energies and beings from the home. Five-pointed borage flowers represent courage. Fleabane daisy, besides repelling insects, symbolizes love and innocence. Bane plants, mentioned earlier, are great for bindings, removing baleful influences, and repelling hexes. Hazel wands, placed at the perimeter of a magick circle or in the corners of a home, are protective. Eyebright, besides having curative properties, can assist with clairvoyance. The sweet fragrance of lilacs can be used as an aphrodisiac. Heliotrope and morning glory represent the sun and moon, respectively. Read books on mythology to find plants that represent various deities and entities.

Wishing you happy herbcrafting, and Bendythion!

**A.C. Fisher Aldag** *(Bangor, Michigan) has practiced a folk magico-religion from the British Isles for over forty years. She has assisted in facilitating many local Pagan events and regularly teaches classes and workshops on folk magick. Her book* Common Magick: Origins and Practices of British Folk Magick *is available from Llewellyn.*

**Illustrator: Tim Foley**

# Cannabis and Shadow Work: How to Take a Deeper Dive

Kerri Connor

I must begin with some disclaimers about the intended audience for this article. If you are brand-new to cannabis or shadow work, or both, please go ahead and read this article, as it can give you something to aspire to. But please do *not* attempt the work described here until you have reached the level where you are fully ready for it. Shadow work can create new traumas while revealing repressed memories. You need to be able to handle whatever your higher self

throws at you. It is highly recommended to do shadow work with a mental health professional to help gain the necessary coping skills.

You also want to already be experienced with cannabis and meditating with your high. Certain strains of cannabis may cause anxiety, which is not at all conducive to a meditation session, much less a shadow work session. You need to be fully capable of evaluating your high and knowing how to stay there. My book *Wake, Bake & Meditate* can guide you in learning how to use cannabis for meditation in a peak experience.

In this article I will teach you the benefits of using cannabis for shadow work and a specific meditation to do while you are in a peak experience. When I refer to cannabis here, you will want to be thinking of indica strains. My favorite for meditation work is Northern Lights.

## Benefits of Using Cannabis with Shadow Work

Cannabis is an effective tool in shadow work for multiple reasons. First, for those who use meditation in shadow work (and we know this is where a lot of shadow work takes place), cannabis naturally helps to relax the mind and body, assisting in the meditation process. People who have difficulty focusing their mind can do so much more efficiently with cannabis. It stops the rapid-fire thoughts and lets the mind settle, relax, and focus.

Cannabis helps you to see yourself, and situations, from the more objective yet loving point of view of your higher self. (No pun intended.) It helps activate your higher self and brings down walls that your mind has built. Some of these walls relate to stubbornness; once the wall comes down, you can see other points of view. Some of these walls hold past traumas and regressed memories. Cannabis helps to bring these walls down too. Therefore, it is essential to have coping skills and be able to work with your high instead of against it. Learning traumatic information can cause a flight-or-fight response.

When you are high on cannabis, this trigger can be intensified, which can then produce an anxiety, paranoia, or panic attack. You must be able to control your high by reminding yourself that you are okay. You must be able to cope with an attack or pull yourself out of it. If you are not there yet, that's okay! Keep working toward it, as the end results can be life-changing.

Our minds are incredible, but they are also incredible at protecting us by hiding memories from us. Sometimes the memories are there, but we haven't made the connection from the memories to a past trauma, which now has ramifications in the present and threatens our future. Combining cannabis with your shadow work can help you reveal these traumas and make connections so healing may take place. This is hard work. This is deep hard work. But by being prepared for it, you can successfully uncover a hidden past and begin a journey of healing.

## Peak Experience

A peak experience is the ultimate high. It is the point where the walls between you and the universe shatter. You are one with your higher self, the universe, the Force—whatever you want to call it. It is a moment of pure enlightenment. It is a place where you can see through eyes of objectivity, particularly when looking at yourself. A peak experience is where we commune with our deities, our saints, our spirit guides. It is a temporary nirvana. Here we can also access memories and see them with objectivity, empathy, and compassion.

Some people find it easy to hit a peak; others not so much. For me, since I am also a medical user, I smoke daily. I smoke a lot daily, which means I have a high THC buildup in my system. This also means it takes a lot more THC to get me to a peak experience. I have a much easier time using concentrates (generally a vape oil or live resins) to obtain a peak experience than I do with flower. You will need to experiment to find your own way to your peak. When you hit a peak, you know it. If you are still questioning if you are there, yet, you aren't. Once you can obtain the peak experience, you will be able to move on to perform the meditation in this article. Even if you cannot fully reach a peak yet, the exercise at the beginning of this meditation may give you enough of a boost to hit it.

## Let's Get Ready to Meditate

I do most of my meditating in the hot tub. Being able to float, weightlessly, while high, and especially when I can do it at night, is a spiritual experience all its own. Do what you need to be safe and comfortable. I recommend lying down over sitting, as it is more relaxing. Allowing your physical body to "float" as much as possible helps your mind to follow suit. You may want a blanket, pillow, bolster, water bottle, and more cannabis in your chosen form on hand. Ensure that you will not be disturbed, pull up a playlist of songs for meditation, and get comfortable. Remember, throughout this meditation, if you need more cannabis, go ahead and take it! I keep my vape lying on my chest, so not much movement is necessary. Once you become proficient at meditating with cannabis, the act of physically moving to consume more does not interfere with your focus. It becomes natural movement and your mind ignores it.

## Shadow Work: "Why?" Meditation

Begin this meditation by taking several deep breaths and allowing yourself to relax. Feel the THC in your system working with you to relax and lift your vibrations.

To help make the connection to your higher self, allow a thought to come into your mind, then step back. Witness yourself having that thought. Say to yourself, "I can see myself thinking." When you do this, you help separate your higher self from your thinking self. This assists you in hitting that state of oneness with the universe. Throughout this meditation, you will be working through this higher self.

When you feel yourself hitting the desired state of mind/spirit, think of a negative trait of yours that you wish to eliminate. What is something you do that you know is wrong but cannot seem to stop yourself from doing? Conjure in your mind the way this trait has affected not only you, but also the people you have loved in your life. Recall different incidents when you exhibited this trait. Even though you know these moments caused pain, for now, let your higher self see them objectively. There is no judgment. Eliminate the emotion surrounding your behavior. See your actions from your higher self's point of view.

Once your higher self fully understands that this is the undesirable trait you want to rid yourself of, and how it has harmed you and others, ask yourself the question "why?" Why did you act this way? Your higher self does not judge, but only gives us facts. Why did you say what you said? Why did you do what you did? The answer will come to you. Your first response may be something like, "I was mad." This is okay. This is only the beginning.

Again, ask yourself, "Why?" This time, ask why you were mad. Listen for your response. "I was mad because I didn't like what so-and-so did."

Your next why question would be "Why did I not like what was done?"

Perhaps your answer is "because they didn't listen to what I said."

Your next question would then be "Why do I get mad when someone doesn't listen to what I say?"

Continue asking yourself why questions, going further and further back with your answer each time. Always turn it back to you, as in asking, "Why do I _______?" Many negative traits can be traced back in time to an unresolved childhood trauma. These traumas have hindered and burdened you. It is time to let them go.

If you hit a roadblock, if you cannot answer a why question, you may very well have repressed memories of unresolved trauma. If this happens, you should speak with your therapist regarding repressed memories. Remember, this meditation may also awaken repressed memories. If your higher self reveals these memories to you, it is time for you to face them. Your higher self knows when you are ready to cope with trauma.

**Remember, this meditation may also awaken repressed memories. If your higher self reveals these memories to you, it is time for you to face them. Your higher self knows when you are ready to cope with trauma.**

When you can trace the behavior back to its origin, you are able to see how these behaviors built up over time, which helps you break the cycle of them continuing. It also provides you with the opportunity to heal this past trauma. You can give yourself now what you did not receive then. Give yourself love and comfort. Give yourself attention and understanding. Heal the childhood trauma that you have carried into adulthood. Understand that the trauma was not your fault. You were not to blame. Once you sense that the healing has begun and you feel ready, you may end your meditation. You will know when it is time.

Healing this trauma and giving yourself the needed self-care is the first step in changing your patterns of behavior. Once you understand where the negativity came from, it is far easier to control and convert those habits into positive ones.

Working through these traumas in meditation not only reveals their origins, and allows you to heal the trauma, but also lets you decide what new behavior you want to replace the old one with. You get to choose who you are, instead of letting trauma responses decide for you.

This meditation can be done over and over, focusing on different negative traits or habits during each session. It is a deep experience and can leave you feeling both energized and drained at the same time. Part of this is due to the energies you have been connected with, and part of this is because it is simply hard work. This makes it essential to finish off this type of working with some major grounding.

If you can sit directly on the ground, do so. Let the energy seep from you downward into the earth. You can also ground this energy by using some of it up through digesting food. Foods high in fat, such as cheeses and nuts, are perfect for grounding. I love to make up a tray with a variety of foods including nuts, cheese, grapes, olives, crackers, and pickles. Not only does this restore your energy, but it is also another method of self-care. Comfort foods may also be used to ground. When grounding with food, what is most important is how the food makes you feel.

Meditating with cannabis is a deep emotional working that can be used to help us confront, accept, and heal our shadow selves. While it is difficult work, the payoff is a more complete, more healed, more enlightened human being.

You're worth it.

**Kerri Connor** *is the author of* Spells for Tough Times; Wake, Bake & Meditate; 420 Meditations: Enhance Your Spiritual Practice with Cannabis; CBD for Your Health, Mind & Spirit; *and* Spells for Good Times. *She lives in Northern Illinois, where she runs the Gathering Grove and the Spiral Labyrinth.*

**Illustrator: Bri Hermanson**

# How to Apply the Laws and Principles of Magick to Prosperity Workings

Diana Rajchel

Out of all the common things that we turn to magick for, the one that consistently has the lowest reported success is money magick. We cast spells at the right times with the right ingredients, but we don't always get rich beyond our wildest imagination; in fact, we often barely clear what we need to pay our bills, if we see any increase at all. We ask for abundance, and somehow it manifests as more solo socks from the dryer. We ask to prosper, and our social media follower accounts jump, but the financial support fails to rise along with the additional eyeballs.

When it comes to working magick, it seems that paths to money involve the absolute greatest areas of traffic congestion. The bumper-to-bumper traffic isn't due to bottlenecking, even though most certainly several people are trying at once. Unlike a multilane bypass in Los Angeles, there's absolutely room for everyone on the road. When you understand the principles of magick, you will see that the issue of failed money magick is not because of short supply and high demand. Prosperity magick—specifically money magick—tends not to work for the following reasons:

1. Most money magick works with entities that pre-date economics and money as we know them.
2. In the case of animistic practitioners, unless they are spirits that evolved from human-made entities into eternal beings, they will not understand money, although they may well understand abundance.
3. People view money in strange, moralistic ways: we look at it with both desire and shame, then treat it poorly when we manage to get it. Uncomfortable emotional energy and moral discomfort distorts our magical intentions.
4. We use the wrong metaphors for money, which makes it much more difficult to manifest when the poetry of magick converts to the reality of the material plane.

The deities most revered in witchcraft and Pagan traditions often came from agriculture and survival-centered cultures. In the case of animistic spirits, they often don't understand money. When looking at what we have and how we live, these beings look at our collective need for money with confusion. Modern people who have the time and space for a magical practice often already have a home, food, and clean water. To ancient spirits of abundance, this covers their needs.

We have also confused ourselves about money. We now have a morass of tangled ideas and emotions rooted in feelings about deserving or not deserving security and material comfort. Money and prosperity are emotional subjects that we ignore our emotions about, and this often manifests in creating a scarcity mindset that keeps us in a state of struggle.

Money magick does work. To get it to work, you have to change your expectations and understanding of magick.

While no single source lists all the laws and principles of magick, the following ones will help you structure your prosperity spells. They come from Isaac Bonewits's *Authentic Thaumaturgy* and the Hermetic principles according to the *Kybalion*. I focus only on those that can apply to magical workings for raising money. The overview explains each law, suggests ways to apply it, and then suggests an affirmation to align with each law. You can use these affirmations as guidelines in any intention setting you apply to prosperity magick.

## The Law of Knowledge

*The more you know about a given subject, the more control you have over it.*

When crafting prosperity spells, you need to understand money, prosperity, and abundance. People often look at money as something they need more of or as a debt that needs erasure. While both definitions can work well, those who are most successful in working with money understand that currency needs to flow—and that every penny needs a job to do. Because money is abstract, you need to understand it as an energy stream rather than an object. Also, the better you understand money, the better you know what to do with it when it does arrive.

*Affirmation:* I understand money and I know what to do with it.

*Apply it:* Knowledge depends on what you learn and where you are working on your relationship with money. When you begin working money magick, you might need to write affirmations. On the other hand, if you have gotten to the point of regular inflow, you might apply your knowledge to put the money to work for you after it arrives through micro-investments. Start by reading a non-witchcraft article about money management. Then pick an area of concern, such as debt reduction.

## The Law of Cause and Effect

*If the same actions are performed under the same conditions, they will usually be associated with the same or equivalent results.*

In the case of money, if you go to work every day and perform the work you agreed to perform, then you will continue to earn a paycheck (most of the time). Thus, repeating an action with consistency produces an effect. You can apply this to daily, repeated rituals.

*Affirmation:* I have good financial habits and practices.

*Apply it:* You can practice a ritual action intended to attract money, establishing routine spellwork that you repeat on a daily, weekly, or monthly basis. For instance, if once a day you light a stick of incense, sit in meditation, and invite money to come, the energy toward money arriving will build. Then, on a practical level, you can set budgets, spending limits, and spending requirements for yourself as you build savings and take control of how you direct the energy of your money.

## The Law of Contagion

*Objects that come into contact with one another, whether through energy alone or physical touch, can continue to interact after separating.*

For example, if you touch a statue meant to bring money and luck, the energy of that charm interacts with you even after you walk away, until such time that you cut the energetic connection.

*Affirmation:* Contact with money and good fortune lingers on my person.

*Apply it:* This may require using your feet if you want to be "infected" with prosperity. Find a lucky place (for example, a diner called the Lucky Penny) and touch it. While *contagion* often refers to magick that you might want to avoid, such as curses, you can also find bits of luck and prosperity. Look at local folklore for any places that confer blessings, especially financial ones. If you can't locate a specific story about an area, look for the oldest successful retail business near you and touch the door.

## The Law of Words of Power

*If you use the right words the right way, you can make your intentions more effective and powerful. You must understand those words intimately.*

Choose your words with care. *Abundance* versus *prosperity* versus *seventy-five dollars* matters when you craft your spell intention. Look over your intention and its phrasing, and think about the different meanings and interpretations that another person might use.

*Affirmation:* When I call money, it comes to me.

*Apply it:* Write a series of affirmations about receiving money in the way you want to receive it. Use these affirmations as the basis of chants, intention shaping, and sigil creation.

## The Law of Pragmatism

*If it works, it's real enough.*

Money is, in modern society, inherently emotional. When crafting spells to summon it, it's easy to get caught up in doubts and fears—and question if we're "crazy" when we start to see small gains from our persistent workings. Stay firm with yourself when you take on any magical practice. If it works, it works. You need not dilute that success with potential doubts and overthinking.

*Affirmation:* The magick I work for money is effective.

*Apply it:* Whenever it appears that your magick has manifested—whether a new bonus shows up, you have a lucky win, or a class-action lawsuit settlement finds its way to you—accept it. It may help to add an affirmation, such as "I have received and I have room for more," to affirm success to yourself and the money.

## The Law of Unity

*Everything is connected to everything else. All is one.*

I often explain this law by pointing out that everything on Earth comes from something else on Earth. Even if chemically altered, all matter began as something natural. Money is a little unusual in that it is a substance of Earth—all currency comes from material made from the planet—but it is also a substance of ether/a shared idea. It's necessary to bring the idea/etheric energy of money together with its material expression to start it flowing in your direction.

*Affirmation:* I am connected to money by the pathways of Earth and spirit. It is part of them all, and I am part of them all, and through that, we have a connection.

*Apply it:* Find your way of expressing the energy of money (usually something water-based) with a physical expression of currency, whether a check you never cash or a dollar coin. An example of the merging of this energy appears in the Bible. In Matthew 17:27, Jesus tells a disciple to pull a fish out of the lake, and in the fish's mouth is a coin, exactly what he and his disciples needed to pay their taxes that year. If you believe in the view of Jesus as a great magician, consider how he made this spell work. He called upon the connected universe according to the law of unity, and he got a coin (and lunch!) for his efforts.

## The Principle of Correspondence

*As above, so below.*

This principle aligns with the law of unity. Again, the miniature/big metaphor can provide clarity.

Imagine you make a dollhouse designed to match the house you live in. You can alter the energies of the house you live in by making changes to the dollhouse.

*Affirmation:* What I do to make room for money expands into the universe, and money responds by making room to be with me.

*Apply it:* Make a play model of your bank accounts, or a checkbook ledger for them. Then once a day, write a continuously larger number in the ledger or the miniature version of your bank account. When you write the number in the smaller version, the larger version adjusts to fit the shape of what you put forth.

## The Principle of Vibration

*Everything in the universe vibrates or sends out a pulse based on constant motion.*

Atoms constantly move, whether we can perceive them or not. Some mystics talk about raising vibrations beyond the need for money or health, vitality, and union with the divine. All this means is that you match your energy to what it is you want to attract. This is the main principle used by people who like the New Age book *The Secret.*

*Affirmation:* My vibrations draw good to me, and that good includes the money I need for life, pleasure, and security.

*Apply it:* Grab a gold dollar coin or a dollar bill fresh from the bank that has not passed through who knows how many human hands. Using your imagination, visualize the atoms of your body and mind moving at the same speed as the atoms of the dollar. Imagine this every time you perform money-drawing work.

### The Principle of Rhythm

*Everything flows, out and in; everything has its tides; all things rise and fall; the pendulum swing manifests in everything; the measure of the swing to the right is the measure of the swing to the left; rhythm compensates.*

Everything has its cycles. For magick practitioners who use the Bible, it means the same as Ecclesiastes 3:1–8: "For everything there is a season, a time for every activity under heaven. A time to be born and a time to die. A time to plant and a time to harvest." Plan for those cycles and work with, rather than against, the flow of energy.

*Affirmation:* I am in tune with the flow of money; I respect it as it goes, and I welcome it as it comes, as part of its energy stream.

*Apply it:* As silly as it sounds, make yourself a money dance playlist that aligns with the rhythm of the seasons where you live. For example, at what time of year do people slow down where you live? Look at the way money flows in your life during each month of the year, then assemble a playlist that imitates those rhythms. Play this music, or specific songs from it, as you cast your money spells.

These laws and principles are far from exhaustive, and there is no single complete source on the laws of magick. As practitioners, we learn them as we go, and sometimes we think to write down what we figure out and share it with others or refer to old grimoires in which the alchemists and Renaissance-era researchers determined many of them and wrote them down.

I often look to the sources named (Hermetics and Bonewits's *Authentic Thaumaturgy*), and I sometimes take into account the laws of physics, especially the laws of thermodynamics, in my spellcasting. Applying modern science to ritual action often gives me an excuse to add intentional tweaks to my work, especially when an entertaining visual helps me raise energy to direct toward my intention. If I need something to work faster, I heat it. If I need a big energy shift, I look for a way to explode through blocks.

## Putting Understanding into Action

To put these laws and principles into action, you can pull together a large ritual or a series of spells and preparations as you do your greater money working. You may not want to utilize all of them, as that can make spellworking cumbersome. Instead, use the ones that you understand the best to assemble a money-drawing practice for yourself.

For example, according to the law of cause and effect, using cinnamon may work best if you seek money to enhance your ability to go out and see friends. If, however, you want to banish debts, you may find that money arrives more willingly to that end when you burn a bit of goldenseal in a loose incense.

To utilize the principle of correspondence, let's say you want to see your money start pooling and staying with you; you intend to save because your desire for money is about security. You may select a jar or bottle or even work with a live plant such as spearmint that grows easily and abundantly. You may plant the seeds—and pennies in the soil along with it—saying, "As you grow, so does my money, and as this fills my pot, so my bank accounts are filled." Then tend to the plant as you would your money, sometimes trimming down to meet family needs or transplanting as the plant grows larger and you move your money to better-yielding accounts.

As you work this magick over time, the process will become clearer to you—and you will, with continuous effort, see a payoff.

**Diana Rajchel** *began her career planning to serve as clergy and write about all subjects spiritual. It did not occur to her or anyone else to say with what agency she might assume priesthood. The result of this oversight in intention setting is that she is now an itinerant city priestess, well-practiced witch, and somewhat unintentional subversive. Diana splits her time between San Francisco, where she co-owns Golden Apple Metaphysical, and southwestern Michigan, where she runs Earth and Sun spiritual coaching with her partner.*

**Illustrator: Bri Hermanson**

# The Lunar Calendar

## September 2022 to December 2023

SEPTEMBER

| S | M | T | W | T | F | S |
|---|---|---|---|---|---|---|
| | | | | 1 | 2 | 3 |
| 4 | 5 | 6 | 7 | 8 | 9 | 10 |
| 11 | 12 | 13 | 14 | 15 | 16 | 17 |
| 18 | 19 | 20 | 21 | 22 | 23 | 24 |
| 25 | 26 | 27 | 28 | 29 | 30 | |

OCTOBER

| S | M | T | W | T | F | S |
|---|---|---|---|---|---|---|
| | | | | | | 1 |
| 2 | 3 | 4 | 5 | 6 | 7 | 8 |
| 9 | 10 | 11 | 12 | 13 | 14 | 15 |
| 16 | 17 | 18 | 19 | 20 | 21 | 22 |
| 23 | 24 | 25 | 26 | 27 | 28 | 29 |
| 30 | 31 | | | | | |

NOVEMBER

| S | M | T | W | T | F | S |
|---|---|---|---|---|---|---|
| | | 1 | 2 | 3 | 4 | 5 |
| 6 | 7 | 8 | 9 | 10 | 11 | 12 |
| 13 | 14 | 15 | 16 | 17 | 18 | 19 |
| 20 | 21 | 22 | 23 | 24 | 25 | 26 |
| 27 | 28 | 29 | 30 | | | |

DECEMBER

| S | M | T | W | T | F | S |
|---|---|---|---|---|---|---|
| | | | | 1 | 2 | 3 |
| 4 | 5 | 6 | 7 | 8 | 9 | 10 |
| 11 | 12 | 13 | 14 | 15 | 16 | 17 |
| 18 | 19 | 20 | 21 | 22 | 23 | 24 |
| 25 | 26 | 27 | 28 | 29 | 30 | 31 |

## 2023

JANUARY

| S | M | T | W | T | F | S |
|---|---|---|---|---|---|---|
| 1 | 2 | 3 | 4 | 5 | 6 | 7 |
| 8 | 9 | 10 | 11 | 12 | 13 | 14 |
| 15 | 16 | 17 | 18 | 19 | 20 | 21 |
| 22 | 23 | 24 | 25 | 26 | 27 | 28 |
| 29 | 30 | 31 | | | | |

FEBRUARY

| S | M | T | W | T | F | S |
|---|---|---|---|---|---|---|
| | | | 1 | 2 | 3 | 4 |
| 5 | 6 | 7 | 8 | 9 | 10 | 11 |
| 12 | 13 | 14 | 15 | 16 | 17 | 18 |
| 19 | 20 | 21 | 22 | 23 | 24 | 25 |
| 26 | 27 | 28 | | | | |

MARCH

| S | M | T | W | T | F | S |
|---|---|---|---|---|---|---|
| | | | 1 | 2 | 3 | 4 |
| 5 | 6 | 7 | 8 | 9 | 10 | 11 |
| 12 | 13 | 14 | 15 | 16 | 17 | 18 |
| 19 | 20 | 21 | 22 | 23 | 24 | 25 |
| 26 | 27 | 28 | 29 | 30 | 31 | |

APRIL

| S | M | T | W | T | F | S |
|---|---|---|---|---|---|---|
| | | | | | | 1 |
| 2 | 3 | 4 | 5 | 6 | 7 | 8 |
| 9 | 10 | 11 | 12 | 13 | 14 | 15 |
| 16 | 17 | 18 | 19 | 20 | 21 | 22 |
| 23 | 24 | 25 | 26 | 27 | 28 | 29 |
| 30 | | | | | | |

MAY

| S | M | T | W | T | F | S |
|---|---|---|---|---|---|---|
| | 1 | 2 | 3 | 4 | 5 | 6 |
| 7 | 8 | 9 | 10 | 11 | 12 | 13 |
| 14 | 15 | 16 | 17 | 18 | 19 | 20 |
| 21 | 22 | 23 | 24 | 25 | 26 | 27 |
| 28 | 29 | 30 | 31 | | | |

JUNE

| S | M | T | W | T | F | S |
|---|---|---|---|---|---|---|
| | | | | 1 | 2 | 3 |
| 4 | 5 | 6 | 7 | 8 | 9 | 10 |
| 11 | 12 | 13 | 14 | 15 | 16 | 17 |
| 18 | 19 | 20 | 21 | 22 | 23 | 24 |
| 25 | 26 | 27 | 28 | 29 | 30 | |

JULY

| S | M | T | W | T | F | S |
|---|---|---|---|---|---|---|
| | | | | | | 1 |
| 2 | 3 | 4 | 5 | 6 | 7 | 8 |
| 9 | 10 | 11 | 12 | 13 | 14 | 15 |
| 16 | 17 | 18 | 19 | 20 | 21 | 22 |
| 23 | 24 | 25 | 26 | 27 | 28 | 29 |
| 30 | 31 | | | | | |

AUGUST

| S | M | T | W | T | F | S |
|---|---|---|---|---|---|---|
| | | 1 | 2 | 3 | 4 | 5 |
| 6 | 7 | 8 | 9 | 10 | 11 | 12 |
| 13 | 14 | 15 | 16 | 17 | 18 | 19 |
| 20 | 21 | 22 | 23 | 24 | 25 | 26 |
| 27 | 28 | 29 | 30 | 31 | | |

SEPTEMBER

| S | M | T | W | T | F | S |
|---|---|---|---|---|---|---|
| | | | | | 1 | 2 |
| 3 | 4 | 5 | 6 | 7 | 8 | 9 |
| 10 | 11 | 12 | 13 | 14 | 15 | 16 |
| 17 | 18 | 19 | 20 | 21 | 22 | 23 |
| 24 | 25 | 26 | 27 | 28 | 29 | 30 |

OCTOBER

| S | M | T | W | T | F | S |
|---|---|---|---|---|---|---|
| 1 | 2 | 3 | 4 | 5 | 6 | 7 |
| 8 | 9 | 10 | 11 | 12 | 13 | 14 |
| 15 | 16 | 17 | 18 | 19 | 20 | 21 |
| 22 | 23 | 24 | 25 | 26 | 27 | 28 |
| 29 | 30 | 31 | | | | |

NOVEMBER

| S | M | T | W | T | F | S |
|---|---|---|---|---|---|---|
| | | | 1 | 2 | 3 | 4 |
| 5 | 6 | 7 | 8 | 9 | 10 | 11 |
| 12 | 13 | 14 | 15 | 16 | 17 | 18 |
| 19 | 20 | 21 | 22 | 23 | 24 | 25 |
| 26 | 27 | 28 | 29 | 30 | | |

DECEMBER

| S | M | T | W | T | F | S |
|---|---|---|---|---|---|---|
| | | | | | 1 | 2 |
| 3 | 4 | 5 | 6 | 7 | 8 | 9 |
| 10 | 11 | 12 | 13 | 14 | 15 | 16 |
| 17 | 18 | 19 | 20 | 21 | 22 | 23 |
| 24 | 25 | 26 | 27 | 28 | 29 | 30 |
| 31 | | | | | | |

# SEPTEMBER 2022

| SU | M | T | W |
|---|---|---|---|
| 28 | 29 | 30 | 31 |
| 4<br>2nd ♐<br>☽ v/c 9:51 pm<br>☽ → ♑ 10:03 pm | 5<br>2nd ♑<br>♀ → ♍ 12:05 am<br>*Labor Day* | 6<br>2nd ♑<br>☽ v/c 5:43 pm<br>☽ → ♒ 11:41 pm | 7<br>2nd ♒ |
| 11<br>3rd ♓<br>☽ → ♈ 2:47 am | 12<br>3rd ♈ | 13<br>3rd ♈<br>☽ v/c 12:53 am<br>☽ → ♉ 7:39 am | 14<br>3rd ♉ |
| 18<br>4th ♊<br>☽ → ♋ 3:59 am | 19<br>4th ♋ | 20<br>4th ♋<br>☽ v/c 11:57 am<br>☽ → ♌ 4:38 pm | 21<br>4th ♌ |
| ●<br>4th ♍<br>☽ v/c 8:49 am<br>☽ → ♎ 12:43 pm<br>New Moon 5:55 pm<br>*New Moon* | 26<br>1st ♎ | 27<br>1st ♎<br>☽ v/c 12:21 pm<br>☽ → ♏ 7:15 pm | 28<br>1st ♏ |
| 2 | 3 | 4 | 5 |

Eastern Daylight Time (EDT)

**Zodiac Signs**

- ♈ Aries
- ♉ Taurus
- ♊ Gemini
- ♋ Cancer
- ♌ Leo
- ♍ Virgo
- ♎ Libra
- ♏ Scorpio
- ♐ Sagittarius
- ♑ Capricorn
- ♒ Aquarius
- ♓ Pisces

**Planets**

- ☉ Sun
- ☽ Moon
- ☿ Mercury
- ♀ Venus
- ♂ Mars
- ♃ Jupiter
- ♄ Saturn
- ♅ Uranus
- ♆ Neptune
- ♇ Pluto

# SEPTEMBER 2022

| TH | F | SA | NOTES |
|---|---|---|---|
| 1st ♏ 1 | 1st ♏ 2<br>☽ v/c 1:22 pm<br>☽ → ♐ 6:39 pm | 1st ♐ ◐<br>2nd Quarter 2:08 pm | |
| 2nd ♒ 8<br>☽ v/c 8:34 am | 2nd ♒ 9<br>☽ → ♓ 12:42 am<br>☿ ℞ 11:38 pm<br>*Mercury retrograde* | 2nd ♓ ○<br>Full Moon 5:59 am<br>☽ v/c 8:29 pm<br>*Harvest Moon* | |
| 3rd ♉ 15<br>☽ v/c 8:59 am<br>☽ → ♊ 4:16 pm | 3rd ♊ 16 | 3rd ♊ ◑<br>☽ v/c 5:52 pm<br>4th Quarter 5:52 pm | |
| 4th ♌ 22<br>☽ v/c 7:07 am<br>☉ → ♎ 9:04 pm<br>*Mabon*<br>*Sun enters Libra*<br>*Fall Equinox* | 4th ♌ 23<br>☽ → ♍ 3:53 am<br>☿ → ♍ 8:04 am | 4th ♍ 24 | |
| 1st ♏ 29<br>♀ → ♎ 3:49 am<br>☽ v/c 5:20 pm | 1st ♏ 30<br>☽ → ♐ 12:03 am | 1 | |
| 6 | 7 | 8 | |

### Aspects & Moon Phases

| | | | | |
|---|---|---|---|---|
| ☌ Conjunction | 0° | ● New Moon | (1st Quarter) |
| ⚹ Sextile | 60° | ◐ Waxing Moon | (2nd Quarter) |
| □ Square | 90° | ○ Full Moon | (3rd Quarter) |
| △ Trine | 120° | ◑ Waning Moon | (4th Quarter) |
| ⊼ Quincunx | 150° | | |
| ☍ Opposition | 180° | | |

# OCTOBER 2022

| SU | M | T | W |
|---|---|---|---|
| 25 | 26 | 27 | 28 |
| 1st ♐<br>☽ → ♑ 3:38 am<br>☿ D 5:07 am<br>2nd Quarter 8:14 pm<br>◐<br>*Mercury direct* | 3<br>2nd ♑<br>☽ v/c 11:49 pm | 4<br>2nd ♑<br>☽ → ♒ 6:20 am | 5<br>2nd ♒<br>☽ v/c 6:46 pm |
| 2nd ♈<br>Full Moon 4:55 pm<br>○<br>*Blood Moon* | 10<br>3rd ♈<br>☽ v/c 10:02 am<br>☽ → ♉ 5:04 pm<br>☿ → ♎ 7:51 pm | 11<br>3rd ♉ | 12<br>3rd ♉<br>☽ v/c 5:42 pm |
| 16<br>3rd ♋ | 3rd ♋<br>4th Quarter 1:15 pm<br>☽ v/c 4:56 pm<br>◑ | 18<br>4th ♋<br>☽ → ♌ 12:45 am | 19<br>4th ♌ |
| 23<br>4th ♎<br>♄ D 12:07 am<br>♀ → ♏ 3:52 am<br>☉ → ♏ 6:36 am<br>*Sun enters Scorpio* | 24<br>4th ♎<br>☽ v/c 8:36 pm | 4th ♎<br>☽ → ♏ 3:18 am<br>New Moon 6:49 am<br>●<br>*Solar Eclipse/ New Moon* | 26<br>1st ♏ |
| 30<br>1st ♑<br>♂ ℞ 9:26 am<br>*Mars retrograde* | 31<br>1st ♑<br>☽ v/c 11:14 am<br>☽ → ♒ 11:43 am<br>*Samhain*<br>*Halloween* | 1 | 2 |

Eastern Daylight Time (EDT)

## Zodiac Signs

♈ Aries
♉ Taurus
♊ Gemini
♋ Cancer
♌ Leo
♍ Virgo
♎ Libra
♏ Scorpio
♐ Sagittarius
♑ Capricorn
♒ Aquarius
♓ Pisces

## Planets

☉ Sun
☽ Moon
☿ Mercury
♀ Venus
♂ Mars
♃ Jupiter
♄ Saturn
♅ Uranus
♆ Neptune
♇ Pluto

# OCTOBER 2022

| TH | F | SA | NOTES |
|---|---|---|---|
| 29 | 30 | 1st ♐ 1<br>☽ v/c 5:46 pm | |
| 2nd ♒ 6<br>☽ → ♓ 8:47 am | 2nd ♓ 7 | 2nd ♓ 8<br>☽ v/c 7:10 am<br>☽ → ♈ 11:57 am<br>♇ D 5:56 pm | |
| 3rd ♉ 13<br>☽ → ♊ 1:08 am | 3rd ♊ 14 | 3rd ♊ 15<br>☽ v/c 12:11 am<br>☽ → ♋ 12:11 pm | |
| 4th ♌ 20<br>☽ v/c 6:35 am<br>☽ → ♍ 12:25 pm | 4th ♍ 21 | 4th ♍ 22<br>☽ v/c 2:17 pm<br>☽ → ♎ 9:24 pm | |
| 1st ♏ 27<br>☽ v/c 12:27 am<br>☽ → ♐ 6:55 am | 1st ♐ 28<br>♃ → ♓ 1:10 am | 1st ♐ 29<br>☽ v/c 9:10 am<br>☽ → ♑ 9:21 am<br>☿ → ♏ 3:22 pm | |
| 3 | 4 | 5 | |

### Aspects & Moon Phases

|  | |  | |
|---|---|---|---|
| ☌ Conjunction | 0° | ● New Moon | (1st Quarter) |
| ⚹ Sextile | 60° | ◐ Waxing Moon | (2nd Quarter) |
| □ Square | 90° | ○ Full Moon | (3rd Quarter) |
| △ Trine | 120° | ◑ Waning Moon | (4th Quarter) |
| ⚻ Quincunx | 150° | | |
| ☍ Opposition | 180° | | |

# NOVEMBER 2022

| SU | M | T | W |
|---|---|---|---|
| 30 | 31 | 1st ≈≈<br>2nd Quarter 2:37 am ◐ | 2<br>2nd ≈≈<br>☽ v/c 7:08 am<br>☽ → ♓ 2:46 pm |
| 6<br>2nd ♈<br>EST in effect 2:00 am<br>☽ v/c 5:30 pm<br>*Daylight Saving Time ends at 2:00 am* | 7<br>2nd ♈<br>☽ → ♉ 12:15 am | 2nd ♉<br>Full Moon 6:02 am ○<br>*Lunar Eclipse/ Mourning Moon*<br>*Election Day (general)* | 9<br>3rd ♉<br>☽ v/c 7:00 am<br>☽ → ♊ 8:37 am |
| 13<br>3rd ♋ | 14<br>3rd ♋<br>☽ v/c 5:41 am<br>☽ → ♌ 7:48 am | 15<br>3rd ♌ | 3rd ♌<br>♀ → ♐ 1:09 am<br>4th Quarter 8:27 am ◑<br>☽ v/c 6:55 pm<br>☽ → ♍ 8:04 pm |
| 20<br>4th ♎ | 21<br>4th ♎<br>☽ v/c 6:14 am<br>☽ → ♏ 12:16 pm | 22<br>4th ♏<br>☉ → ♐ 3:20 am<br>*Sun enters Sagittarius* | 4th ♏<br>☽ v/c 1:16 pm<br>☽ → ♐ 3:16 pm<br>New Moon 5:57 pm ●<br>♃ D 6:02 pm<br>*New Moon* |
| 27<br>1st ♑<br>☽ v/c 3:11 pm<br>☽ → ≈≈ 5:07 pm | 28<br>1st ≈≈ | 29<br>1st ≈≈<br>☽ v/c 1:53 am<br>☽ → ♓ 7:15 pm | 1st ♓<br>2nd Quarter 9:37 am ◐ |
| 4 | 5 | 6 | 7 |

Eastern Daylight Time (EDT) becomes Eastern Standard Time (EST) November 6

**Zodiac Signs**

♈ Aries ♌ Leo ♐ Sagittarius
♉ Taurus ♍ Virgo ♑ Capricorn
♊ Gemini ♎ Libra ≈≈ Aquarius
♋ Cancer ♏ Scorpio ♓ Pisces

**Planets**

☉ Sun ♃ Jupiter
☽ Moon ♄ Saturn
☿ Mercury ♅ Uranus
♀ Venus ♆ Neptune
♂ Mars ♇ Pluto

# NOVEMBER 2022

| TH | F | SA | NOTES |
|---|---|---|---|
| 2nd ♓ 3 | 2nd ♓ 4<br>☽ v/c 6:05 pm<br>☽ → ♈ 7:07 pm | 2nd ♈ 5 | |
| 3rd ♊ 10 | 3rd ♊ 11<br>☽ v/c 5:28 pm<br>☽ → ♋ 7:22 pm<br>*Veterans Day* | 3rd ♋ 12 | |
| 4th ♍ 17<br>☿ → ♐ 3:42 am | 4th ♍ 18 | 4th ♍ 19<br>☽ v/c 3:47 am<br>☽ → ♎ 5:58 am | |
| 1st ♐ 24<br>*Thanksgiving Day* | 1st ♐ 25<br>☽ v/c 2:22 pm<br>☽ → ♑ 4:18 pm | 1st ♑ 26 | |
| 1 | 2 | 3 | |
| 8 | 9 | 10 | |

## Aspects & Moon Phases

|  |  |  |  |
|---|---|---|---|
| ☌ Conjunction | 0° | ● New Moon | (1st Quarter) |
| ⚹ Sextile | 60° | ◐ Waxing Moon | (2nd Quarter) |
| □ Square | 90° | ○ Full Moon | (3rd Quarter) |
| △ Trine | 120° | ◑ Waning Moon | (4th Quarter) |
| ⚻ Quincunx | 150° | | |
| ☍ Opposition | 180° | | |

# DECEMBER 2022

| SU | M | T | W |
|---|---|---|---|
| 27 | 28 | 29 | 30 |
| 4<br>2nd ♈<br>☽ v/c 12:46 am<br>☽ → ♉ 6:38 am | 5<br>2nd ♉ | 6<br>2nd ♉<br>☽ v/c 2:02 pm<br>☽ → ♊ 3:49 pm<br>☿ → ♑ 5:08 pm | ○<br>2nd ♊<br>Full Moon 11:08 pm<br>*Long Nights Moon* |
| 11<br>3rd ♋<br>☽ v/c 1:49 pm<br>☽ → ♌ 3:09 pm | 12<br>3rd ♌ | 13<br>3rd ♌<br>☽ v/c 10:52 am | 14<br>3rd ♌<br>☽ → ♍ 3:45 am |
| 18<br>4th ♎<br>☽ v/c 5:35 pm<br>☽ → ♏ 10:31 pm | 19<br>4th ♏ | 20<br>4th ♏<br>♃ → ♈ 9:32 am<br>☽ v/c 9:45 pm | 21<br>4th ♏<br>☽ → ♐ 2:12 am<br>☉ → ♑ 4:48 pm<br>*Yule*<br>*Sun enters Capricorn*<br>*Winter Solstice* |
| 25<br>1st ♑<br>☽ → ♒ 2:14 am<br>*Christmas Day* | 26<br>1st ♒<br>☽ v/c 1:19 pm<br>*Kwanzaa begins* | 27<br>1st ♒<br>☽ → ♓ 2:34 am | 28<br>1st ♓ |
| 1 | 2 | 3 | 4 |

Eastern Standard Time (EST)

**Zodiac Signs**

♈ Aries ♌ Leo ♐ Sagittarius
♉ Taurus ♍ Virgo ♑ Capricorn
♊ Gemini ♎ Libra ♒ Aquarius
♋ Cancer ♏ Scorpio ♓ Pisces

**Planets**

☉ Sun ♃ Jupiter
☽ Moon ♄ Saturn
☿ Mercury ♅ Uranus
♀ Venus ♆ Neptune
♂ Mars ♇ Pluto

# DECEMBER 2022

| TH | F | SA | NOTES |
|---|---|---|---|
| **1** 2nd ♓ ☽ v/c 9:44 pm ☽ → ♈ 11:41 pm | **2** 2nd ♈ | **3** 2nd ♈ ♆ D 7:15 pm | |
| **8** 3rd ♊ | **9** 3rd ♊ ☽ v/c 1:13 am ☽ → ♋ 2:49 am ♀ → ♑ 10:54 pm | **10** 3rd ♋ | |
| **15** 3rd ♍ | **16** ◑ 3rd ♍ 4th Quarter 3:56 am ☽ v/c 2:13 pm ☽ → ♎ 2:49 pm | **17** 4th ♎ | |
| **22** 4th ♐ ☽ v/c 3:16 pm | **23** ● 4th ♐ ☽ → ♑ 2:49 am New Moon 5:17 am *New Moon* | **24** 1st ♑ ☽ v/c 10:11 pm *Christmas Eve* | |
| **29** ◐ 1st ♓ ☽ v/c 1:21 am ☿ ℞ 4:32 am ☽ → ♈ 5:36 am 2nd Quarter 8:21 pm *Mercury retrograde* | **30** 2nd ♈ | **31** 2nd ♈ ☽ v/c 7:44 am ☽ → ♉ 12:08 pm *New Year's Eve* | |
| 5 | 6 | 7 | |

Aspects & Moon Phases

| | | | | |
|---|---|---|---|---|
| ☌ Conjunction | 0° | | ● New Moon | (1st Quarter) |
| ⚹ Sextile | 60° | | ◐ Waxing Moon | (2nd Quarter) |
| □ Square | 90° | | ○ Full Moon | (3rd Quarter) |
| △ Trine | 120° | | ◑ Waning Moon | (4th Quarter) |
| ⚻ Quincunx | 150° | | | |
| ☍ Opposition | 180° | | | |

# JANUARY 2023

| SU | M | T | W |
|---|---|---|---|
| 2nd ♉ **1**<br><br>*New Year's Day* | 2nd ♉ **2**<br>☽ v/c 5:16 pm<br>♀ → ♒ 9:09 pm<br>☽ → ♊ 9:44 pm | 2nd ♊ **3** | 2nd ♊ **4**<br>☽ v/c 7:08 pm |
| 3rd ♌ **8** | 3rd ♌ **9**<br>☽ v/c 8:52 pm | 3rd ♌ **10**<br>☽ → ♍ 10:15 am | 3rd ♍ **11** |
| 4th ♎ **15**<br>☽ v/c 3:40 am<br>☽ → ♏ 7:08 am | 4th ♏ **16**<br><br>*Martin Luther King Jr. Day* | 4th ♏ **17**<br>☽ v/c 9:27 am<br>☽ → ♐ 12:33 pm | 4th ♐ **18**<br>☿ D 8:12 am<br><br>*Mercury direct* |
| 1st ♒ **22**<br>♅ D 5:59 pm<br><br>*Lunar New Year (Rabbit)* | 1st ♒ **23**<br>☽ v/c 5:19 am<br>☽ → ♓ 12:36 pm | 1st ♓ **24** | 1st ♓ **25**<br>☽ v/c 11:12 am<br>☽ → ♈ 1:48 pm |
| 2nd ♉ **29** | 2nd ♉ **30**<br>☽ v/c 12:52 am<br>☽ → ♊ 3:35 am | 2nd ♊ **31** | 1 |
| 5 | 6 | 7 | 8 |

Eastern Standard Time (EST)

**Zodiac Signs**

♈ Aries
♉ Taurus
♊ Gemini
♋ Cancer
♌ Leo
♍ Virgo
♎ Libra
♏ Scorpio
♐ Sagittarius
♑ Capricorn
♒ Aquarius
♓ Pisces

**Planets**

☉ Sun
☽ Moon
☿ Mercury
♀ Venus
♂ Mars
♃ Jupiter
♄ Saturn
♅ Uranus
♆ Neptune
♇ Pluto

# JANUARY 2023

| TH | F | SA | NOTES |
|---|---|---|---|
| **5** 2nd ♊ ☽ → ♋ 9:15 am | **6** ○ 2nd ♋ Full Moon 6:08 pm *Cold Moon* | **7** 3rd ♋ ☽ v/c 5:23 pm ☽ → ♌ 9:40 pm | |
| **12** 3rd ♍ ♂ D 3:56 pm ☽ v/c 6:06 pm ☽ → ♎ 9:56 pm *Mars direct* | **13** 3rd ♎ | **14** ◑ 3rd ♎ 4th Quarter 9:10 pm | |
| **19** 4th ♐ ☽ v/c 5:09 am ☽ → ♑ 2:11 pm | **20** 4th ♑ ☉ → ♒ 3:30 am *Sun enters Aquarius* | **21** ● 4th ♑ ☽ v/c 10:52 am ☽ → ♒ 1:29 pm New Moon 3:53 pm *New Moon* | |
| **26** 1st ♈ ♀ → ♓ 9:33 pm | **27** 1st ♈ ☽ v/c 4:01 pm ☽ → ♉ 6:42 pm | **28** ◐ 1st ♉ 2nd Quarter 10:19 am | |
| 2 | 3 | 4 | |
| 9 | 10 | 11 | |

Aspects & Moon Phases

|  |  |  |  |
|---|---|---|---|
| ☌ Conjunction | 0° | ● New Moon | (1st Quarter) |
| ⚹ Sextile | 60° | ◐ Waxing Moon | (2nd Quarter) |
| □ Square | 90° | ○ Full Moon | (3rd Quarter) |
| △ Trine | 120° | ◑ Waning Moon | (4th Quarter) |
| ⚻ Quincunx | 150° | | |
| ☍ Opposition | 180° | | |

# FEBRUARY 2023

| SU | M | T | W |
|---|---|---|---|
| 29 | 30 | 31 | 2nd ♊ 1<br>☽ v/c 6:58 am<br>☽ → ♋ 3:11 pm |
| 2nd ♌ ○<br>Full Moon 1:29 pm<br>*Quickening Moon* | 3rd ♌ 6<br>☽ v/c 9:15 am<br>☽ → ♍ 4:14 pm | 3rd ♍ 7 | 3rd ♍ 8 |
| 3rd ♏ 12 | 3rd ♏ ◑<br>4th Quarter 11:01 am<br>☽ v/c 6:52 pm<br>☽ → ♐ 8:31 pm | 4th ♐ 14<br>*Valentine's Day* | 4th ♐ 15<br>☽ v/c 8:06 pm |
| 4th ♒ 19<br>☽ v/c 9:00 pm<br>☽ → ♓ 11:56 pm | 4th ♓ ●<br>New Moon 2:06 am<br>♀ → ♈ 2:56 am<br>*Presidents' Day*<br>*New Moon* | 1st ♓ 21<br>☽ v/c 11:06 pm<br>*Mardi Gras (Fat Tuesday)* | 1st ♓ 22<br>☽ → ♈ 12:14 am<br>*Ash Wednesday* |
| 1st ♉ 26<br>☽ v/c 9:42 am<br>☽ → ♊ 10:48 am | 1st ♊ ◐<br>2nd Quarter 3:06 am | 2nd ♊ 28<br>☽ v/c 8:07 pm<br>☽ → ♋ 9:40 pm | 1 |
| 5 | 6 | 7 | 8 |

Eastern Standard Time (EST)

**Zodiac Signs**

♈ Aries
♉ Taurus
♊ Gemini
♋ Cancer
♌ Leo
♍ Virgo
♎ Libra
♏ Scorpio
♐ Sagittarius
♑ Capricorn
♒ Aquarius
♓ Pisces

**Planets**

☉ Sun
☽ Moon
☿ Mercury
♀ Venus
♂ Mars
♃ Jupiter
♄ Saturn
♅ Uranus
♆ Neptune
♇ Pluto

# FEBRUARY 2023

| TH | F | SA | NOTES |
|---|---|---|---|
| 2nd ♋ 2<br><br>*Imbolc*<br>*Groundhog Day* | 2nd ♋ 3 | 2nd ♋ 4<br>☽ v/c 1:19 am<br>☽ → ♌ 3:48 am | |
| 3rd ♍ 9<br>☽ v/c 1:40 am<br>☽ → ♎ 3:47 am | 3rd ♎ 10 | 3rd ♎ 11<br>☿ → ♒ 6:22 am<br>☽ v/c 11:41 am<br>☽ → ♏ 1:34 pm | |
| 4th ♑ 16<br>☽ → ♑ 12:00 am | 4th ♑ 17<br>☽ v/c 11:18 pm | 4th ♑ 18<br>☽ → ♒ 12:35 am<br>☉ → ♓ 5:34 pm<br><br>*Sun enters Pisces* | |
| 1st ♈ 23 | 1st ♈ 24<br>☽ v/c 2:22 am<br>☽ → ♉ 3:29 am | 1st ♉ 25 | |
| 2 | 3 | 4 | |
| 9 | 10 | 11 | |

### Aspects & Moon Phases

|  |  |  |
|---|---|---|
| ☌ | Conjunction | 0° |
| ✶ | Sextile | 60° |
| □ | Square | 90° |
| △ | Trine | 120° |
| ⚻ | Quincunx | 150° |
| ☍ | Opposition | 180° |

|  |  |  |
|---|---|---|
| ● | New Moon | (1st Quarter) |
| ◐ | Waxing Moon | (2nd Quarter) |
| ○ | Full Moon | (3rd Quarter) |
| ◑ | Waning Moon | (4th Quarter) |

# MARCH 2023

| SU | M | T | W |
|---|---|---|---|
| 26 | 27 | 28 | 2nd ♋ 1 |
| 2nd ♌<br>☽ v/c 10:18 pm<br>☽ → ♍ 10:38 pm 5 | 2nd ♍ 6 | 2nd ♍ ○<br>Full Moon 7:40 am<br>♄ → ♓ 8:35 am<br>*Storm Moon* 7 | 3rd ♍ 8<br>☽ v/c 9:07 am<br>☽ → ♎ 9:44 am |
| 3rd ♏ 12<br>EDT in effect 2:00 am<br>*Daylight Saving Time begins at 2:00 am* | 3rd ♏ 13<br>☽ v/c 2:58 am<br>☽ → ♐ 3:21 am | 3rd ♐ ◑<br>4th Quarter 10:08 pm 14 | 4th ♐ 15<br>☽ v/c 4:50 am<br>☽ → ♑ 8:06 am |
| 4th ♒ 19<br>☿ → ♈ 12:24 am<br>☽ v/c 6:33 am<br>☽ → ♓ 11:12 am | 4th ♓ 20<br>☉ → ♈ 5:24 pm<br>*Ostara*<br>*Sun enters Aries*<br>*Spring Equinox* | 4th ♓ ●<br>☽ v/c 11:58 am<br>☽ → ♈ 12:01 pm<br>New Moon 1:23 pm<br>*New Moon* 21 | 1st ♈ 22 |
| 1st ♊ 26 | 1st ♊ 27<br>☽ v/c 9:39 pm | 1st ♊ ◐<br>☽ → ♋ 6:22 am<br>2nd Quarter 10:32 pm 28 | 2nd ♋ 29 |
| 2 | 3 | 4 | 5 |

Eastern Standard Time (EST) becomes Eastern Daylight Time (EDT) March 12

**Zodiac Signs**

♈ Aries ♉ Taurus ♊ Gemini ♋ Cancer ♌ Leo ♍ Virgo ♎ Libra ♏ Scorpio ♐ Sagittarius ♑ Capricorn ♒ Aquarius ♓ Pisces

**Planets**

☉ Sun ☽ Moon ☿ Mercury ♀ Venus ♂ Mars ♃ Jupiter ♄ Saturn ♅ Uranus ♆ Neptune ♇ Pluto

# MARCH 2023

| TH | F | SA | NOTES |
|---|---|---|---|
| 2nd ♋ 2<br>☿ → ♓ 5:52 pm | 2nd ♋ 3<br>☽ v/c 9:22 am<br>☽ → ♌ 10:16 am | 2nd ♌ 4 | |
| 3rd ♎ 9 | 3rd ♎ 10<br>☽ v/c 6:37 pm<br>☽ → ♏ 7:06 pm | 3rd ♏ 11 | |
| 4th ♑ 16<br>♀ → ♉ 6:34 pm | 4th ♑ 17<br>☽ v/c 10:14 am<br>☽ → ♒ 10:25 am<br>*St. Patrick's Day* | 4th ♒ 18 | |
| 1st ♈ 23<br>♇ → ♒ 8:13 am<br>☽ v/c 1:13 pm<br>☽ → ♉ 2:42 pm | 1st ♉ 24 | 1st ♉ 25<br>♂ → ♋ 7:45 am<br>☽ v/c 12:19 pm<br>☽ → ♊ 8:42 pm | |
| 2nd ♋ 30<br>☽ v/c 9:45 am<br>☽ → ♌ 6:31 pm | 2nd ♌ 31 | 1 | |
| 6 | 7 | 8 | |

### Aspects & Moon Phases

|  |  |  |  |
|---|---|---|---|
| ☌ Conjunction | 0° | ● New Moon | (1st Quarter) |
| ⚹ Sextile | 60° | ◐ Waxing Moon | (2nd Quarter) |
| □ Square | 90° | ○ Full Moon | (3rd Quarter) |
| △ Trine | 120° | ◑ Waning Moon | (4th Quarter) |
| ⚻ Quincunx | 150° | | |
| ☍ Opposition | 180° | | |

# APRIL 2023

| SU | M | T | W |
|---|---|---|---|
| 26 | 27 | 28 | 29 |
| 2<br>2nd ♌<br>☽ v/c 2:03 am<br>☽ → ♍ 6:57 am | 3<br>2nd ♍<br>☿ → ♉ 12:22 pm | 4<br>2nd ♍<br>☽ v/c 9:50 am<br>☽ → ♎ 5:51 pm | 5<br>2nd ♎ |
| 9<br>3rd ♏<br>☽ v/c 5:09 am<br>☽ → ♐ 8:57 am<br>*Easter* | 10<br>3rd ♐ | 11<br>3rd ♐<br>♀ → ♊ 12:47 am<br>☽ v/c 6:48 am<br>☽ → ♑ 1:33 pm | 12<br>3rd ♑ |
| 16<br>4th ♓ | 17<br>4th ♓<br>☽ v/c 2:57 pm<br>☽ → ♈ 9:09 pm | 18<br>4th ♈ | 19<br>4th ♈ |
| 23<br>1st ♊ | 24<br>1st ♊<br>☽ v/c 8:15 am<br>☽ → ♋ 2:58 pm | 25<br>1st ♋ | 26<br>1st ♋<br>☽ v/c 7:41 pm |
| 30<br>2nd ♍ | 1 | 2 | 3 |

Eastern Daylight Time (EDT)

**Zodiac Signs**

♈ Aries
♉ Taurus
♊ Gemini
♋ Cancer
♌ Leo
♍ Virgo
♎ Libra
♏ Scorpio
♐ Sagittarius
♑ Capricorn
♒ Aquarius
♓ Pisces

**Planets**

☉ Sun
☽ Moon
☿ Mercury
♀ Venus
♂ Mars
♃ Jupiter
♄ Saturn
♅ Uranus
♆ Neptune
♇ Pluto

# APRIL 2023

| TH | F | SA | NOTES |
|---|---|---|---|
| 30 | 31 | 2nd ♌ 1<br>*All Fools' Day* | |
| 2nd ♎ ○<br>Full Moon 12:34 am<br>☽ v/c 8:43 am<br>*Wind Moon* | 3rd ♎ 7<br>☽ → ♏ 2:29 am<br>*Good Friday* | 3rd ♏ 8 | |
| 3rd ♑ ◑<br>4th Quarter 5:11 am<br>☽ v/c 10:14 am<br>☽ → ♒ 4:42 pm | 4th ♒ 14 | 4th ♒ 15<br>☽ v/c 11:16 am<br>☽ → ♓ 6:57 pm | |
| 4th ♈ ●<br>☽ v/c 12:13 am<br>New Moon 12:13 am<br>☽ → ♉ 12:30 am<br>☉ → ♉ 4:14 am<br>*Sun enters Taurus*<br>*Solar Eclipse/New Moon* | 1st ♉ 21<br>☿ ℞ 4:35 am<br>☽ v/c 11:41 pm<br>*Mercury retrograde* | 1st ♉ 22<br>☽ → ♊ 6:11 am<br>*Earth Day* | |
| 1st ♋ ◐<br>☽ → ♌ 2:30 am<br>2nd Quarter 5:20 pm | 2nd ♌ 28 | 2nd ♌ 29<br>☽ v/c 6:53 am<br>☽ → ♍ 2:59 pm | |
| 4 | 5 | 6 | |

### Aspects & Moon Phases

| | | | |
|---|---|---|---|
| ☌ Conjunction | 0° | ● New Moon | (1st Quarter) |
| ✶ Sextile | 60° | ◐ Waxing Moon | (2nd Quarter) |
| □ Square | 90° | ○ Full Moon | (3rd Quarter) |
| △ Trine | 120° | ◑ Waning Moon | (4th Quarter) |
| ⊼ Quincunx | 150° | | |
| ☍ Opposition | 180° | | |

# MAY 2023

| SU | M | T | W |
|---|---|---|---|
| 30 | 1<br>2nd ♍<br>♇ ℞ 1:09 pm<br>☽ v/c 7:53 pm<br>*Beltane* | 2<br>2nd ♍<br>☽ → ♎ 2:09 am | 3<br>2nd ♎ |
| 7<br>3rd ♐<br>♀ → ♋ 10:25 am | 8<br>3rd ♐<br>☽ v/c 4:28 pm<br>☽ → ♑ 7:33 pm | 9<br>3rd ♑ | 10<br>3rd ♑<br>☽ v/c 7:52 pm<br>☽ → ♒ 10:05 pm |
| 14<br>4th ♓<br>☽ v/c 10:56 pm<br>☿ D 11:17 pm<br>*Mother's Day*<br>*Mercury direct* | 15<br>4th ♓<br>☽ → ♈ 3:56 am | 16<br>4th ♈<br>♃ → ♉ 1:20 pm | 17<br>4th ♈<br>☽ v/c 5:10 am<br>☽ → ♉ 8:28 am |
| 21<br>1st ♊<br>☉ → ♊ 3:09 am<br>☽ v/c 6:12 pm<br>☽ → ♋ 11:28 pm<br>*Sun enters Gemini* | 22<br>1st ♋ | 23<br>1st ♋ | 24<br>1st ♋<br>☽ v/c 5:12 am<br>☽ → ♌ 10:35 am |
| 28<br>2nd ♍ | 29<br>2nd ♍<br>☽ v/c 5:46 am<br>☽ → ♎ 10:51 am<br>*Memorial Day* | 30<br>2nd ♎ | 31<br>2nd ♎<br>☽ v/c 10:53 am<br>☽ → ♏ 7:45 pm |
| 4 | 5 | 6 | 7 |

Eastern Daylight Time (EDT)

**Zodiac Signs**

♈ Aries
♉ Taurus
♊ Gemini
♋ Cancer
♌ Leo
♍ Virgo
♎ Libra
♏ Scorpio
♐ Sagittarius
♑ Capricorn
♒ Aquarius
♓ Pisces

**Planets**

☉ Sun
☽ Moon
☿ Mercury
♀ Venus
♂ Mars
♃ Jupiter
♄ Saturn
♅ Uranus
♆ Neptune
♇ Pluto

# MAY 2023

| TH | F | SA | NOTES |
|---|---|---|---|
| 2nd ♎ 4<br>☽ v/c 5:17 am<br>☽ → ♏ 10:32 am | 2nd ♏ ○<br>Full Moon 1:34 pm<br>*Lunar Eclipse/ Flower Moon* | 3rd ♏ 6<br>☽ v/c 10:38 am<br>☽ → ♐ 4:04 pm | |
| 3rd ♒ 11 | 3rd ♒ ◑<br>4th Quarter 10:28 am<br>☽ v/c 11:15 pm | 4th ♒ 13<br>☽ → ♓ 12:39 am | |
| 4th ♉ 18 | 4th ♉ ●<br>New Moon 11:53 am<br>☽ v/c 1:51 pm<br>☽ → ♊ 2:48 pm<br>*New Moon* | 1st ♊ 20<br>♂ → ♌ 11:31 am | |
| 1st ♌ 25 | 1st ♌ 26<br>☽ v/c 2:38 am<br>☽ → ♍ 11:05 pm | 1st ♍ ◐<br>2nd Quarter 11:22 am | |
| 1 | 2 | 3 | |
| 8 | 9 | 10 | |

Aspects & Moon Phases

|  |  |  |  |
|---|---|---|---|
| ☌ Conjunction | 0° | ● New Moon | (1st Quarter) |
| ✶ Sextile | 60° | ◐ Waxing Moon | (2nd Quarter) |
| □ Square | 90° | ○ Full Moon | (3rd Quarter) |
| △ Trine | 120° | ◑ Waning Moon | (4th Quarter) |
| ⊼ Quincunx | 150° | | |
| ☍ Opposition | 180° | | |

# JUNE 2023

| SU | M | T | W |
|---|---|---|---|
| 28 | 29 | 30 | 31 |
| 4<br>3rd ♐<br>☽ v/c 11:24 pm | 5<br>3rd ♐<br>☽ → ♑ 3:31 am<br>♀ → ♌ 9:46 am | 6<br>3rd ♑ | 7<br>3rd ♑<br>☽ v/c 12:40 am<br>☽ → ♒ 4:42 am |
| 11<br>4th ♓<br>♇ → ♑ 5:47 am<br>☿ → ♊ 6:27 am<br>☽ v/c 9:20 am<br>☽ → ♈ 9:20 am | 12<br>4th ♈ | 13<br>4th ♈<br>☽ v/c 2:27 pm<br>☽ → ♉ 2:31 pm | 14<br>4th ♉ |
| ●<br>4th ♊<br>New Moon 12:37 am<br>☽ v/c 2:24 am<br>☽ → ♋ 6:58 am<br>*Father's Day*<br>*Juneteenth*<br>*New Moon* | 19<br>1st ♋ | 20<br>1st ♋<br>☽ v/c 5:43 pm<br>☽ → ♌ 6:04 pm | 21<br>1st ♌<br>☉ → ♋ 10:58 am<br>*Litha*<br>*Sun enters Cancer*<br>*Summer Solstice* |
| 25<br>1st ♍<br>☽ v/c 6:24 pm<br>☽ → ♎ 6:57 pm | ◐<br>1st ♎<br>2nd Quarter 3:50 am<br>☿ → ♋ 8:24 pm | 27<br>2nd ♎ | 28<br>2nd ♎<br>☽ v/c 4:19 am<br>☽ → ♏ 4:55 am |
| 2 | 3 | 4 | 5 |

Eastern Daylight Time (EDT)

### Zodiac Signs

♈ Aries
♉ Taurus
♊ Gemini
♋ Cancer
♌ Leo
♍ Virgo
♎ Libra
♏ Scorpio
♐ Sagittarius
♑ Capricorn
♒ Aquarius
♓ Pisces

### Planets

☉ Sun
☽ Moon
☿ Mercury
♀ Venus
♂ Mars
♃ Jupiter
♄ Saturn
♅ Uranus
♆ Neptune
♇ Pluto

# JUNE 2023

| TH | F | SA | NOTES |
|---|---|---|---|
| 2nd ♏ 1 | 2nd ♏ 2<br>☽ v/c 8:51 pm | 2nd ♏ ○<br>☽ → ♐ 1:03 am<br>Full Moon 11:42 pm<br>*Strong Sun Moon* | |
| 3rd ♒ 8 | 3rd ♒ 9<br>☽ v/c 12:24 am<br>☽ → ♓ 6:14 am | 3rd ♓ ◑<br>4th Quarter 3:31 pm | |
| 4th ♉ 15<br>☽ v/c 9:36 pm<br>☽ → ♊ 9:40 pm | 4th ♊ 16 | 4th ♊ 17<br>♄ ℞ 1:27 pm | |
| 1st ♌ 22<br>☽ v/c 1:01 pm | 1st ♌ 23<br>☽ → ♍ 6:35 am | 1st ♍ 24 | |
| 2nd ♏ 29 | 2nd ♏ 30<br>☽ v/c 10:20 am<br>☽ → ♐ 10:59 am<br>♆ ℞ 5:07 pm | 1 | |
| 6 | 7 | 8 | |

### Aspects & Moon Phases

| | | | |
|---|---|---|---|
| ☌ Conjunction | 0° | ● New Moon | (1st Quarter) |
| ✳ Sextile | 60° | ◐ Waxing Moon | (2nd Quarter) |
| □ Square | 90° | ○ Full Moon | (3rd Quarter) |
| △ Trine | 120° | ◑ Waning Moon | (4th Quarter) |
| ⚻ Quincunx | 150° | | |
| ☍ Opposition | 180° | | |

# JULY 2023

| SU | M | T | W |
|---|---|---|---|
| 25 | 26 | 27 | 28 |
| 2<br>2nd ♐<br>☽ v/c 9:33 am<br>☽ → ♑ 1:20 pm | 3<br>2nd ♑<br>Full Moon 7:39 am<br>*Blessing Moon* | 4<br>3rd ♑<br>☽ v/c 12:45 pm<br>☽ → ♒ 1:30 pm<br>*Independence Day* | 5<br>3rd ♒ |
| 9<br>3rd ♈<br>4th Quarter 9:48 pm | 10<br>4th ♈<br>♂ → ♍ 7:40 am<br>☽ v/c 7:11 pm<br>☽ → ♉ 7:55 pm | 11<br>4th ♉<br>☿ → ♌ 12:11 am | 12<br>4th ♉ |
| 16<br>4th ♋ | 17<br>4th ♋<br>New Moon 2:32 pm<br>☽ v/c 11:06 pm<br>*New Moon* | 18<br>1st ♋<br>☽ → ♌ 12:39 am | 19<br>1st ♌ |
| 23<br>1st ♍<br>☽ v/c 12:06 am<br>☽ → ♎ 1:54 am | 24<br>1st ♎ | 25<br>1st ♎<br>☽ v/c 11:05 am<br>☽ → ♏ 12:55 pm<br>2nd Quarter 6:07 pm | 26<br>2nd ♏ |
| 30<br>2nd ♑ | 31<br>2nd ♑<br>☽ v/c 10:13 pm<br>☽ → ♒ 11:58 pm | 1 | 2 |

Eastern Daylight Time (EDT)

**Zodiac Signs**

♈ Aries ♉ Taurus ♊ Gemini ♋ Cancer ♌ Leo ♍ Virgo ♎ Libra ♏ Scorpio ♐ Sagittarius ♑ Capricorn ♒ Aquarius ♓ Pisces

**Planets**

☉ Sun ☽ Moon ☿ Mercury ♀ Venus ♂ Mars ♃ Jupiter ♄ Saturn ♅ Uranus ♆ Neptune ♇ Pluto

# JULY 2023

| TH | F | SA | NOTES |
|---|---|---|---|
| 29 | 30 | 1<br>2nd ♐ | |
| 6<br>3rd ♒<br>☽ v/c 9:42 am<br>☽ → ♓ 1:33 pm | 7<br>3rd ♓ | 8<br>3rd ♓<br>☽ v/c 2:22 pm<br>☽ → ♈ 3:19 pm | |
| 13<br>4th ♉<br>☽ v/c 2:11 am<br>☽ → ♊ 3:26 am | 14<br>4th ♊ | 15<br>4th ♊<br>☽ v/c 8:35 am<br>☽ → ♋ 1:13 pm | |
| 20<br>1st ♌<br>☽ v/c 10:08 am<br>☽ → ♍ 1:13 pm | 21<br>1st ♍ | 22<br>1st ♍<br>♀ ℞ 9:33 pm<br>☉ → ♌ 9:50 pm<br>*Sun enters Leo* | |
| 27<br>2nd ♏<br>☽ v/c 6:30 pm<br>☽ → ♐ 8:24 pm | 28<br>2nd ♐<br>☿ → ♍ 5:31 pm | 29<br>2nd ♐<br>☽ v/c 7:51 pm<br>☽ → ♑ 11:44 pm | |
| 3 | 4 | 5 | |

**Aspects & Moon Phases**

|  |  |  |  |
|---|---|---|---|
| ☌ Conjunction | 0° | ● New Moon | (1st Quarter) |
| ⚹ Sextile | 60° | ◐ Waxing Moon | (2nd Quarter) |
| □ Square | 90° | ○ Full Moon | (3rd Quarter) |
| △ Trine | 120° | ◑ Waning Moon | (4th Quarter) |
| ⚻ Quincunx | 150° | | |
| ☍ Opposition | 180° | | |

# AUGUST 2023

| SU | M | T | W |
|---|---|---|---|
| 30 | 31 | 2nd ≈ Full Moon 2:32 pm ○ *Lammas* *Corn Moon* | 2 3rd ≈ ☽ v/c 5:15 pm ☽ → ♓ 11:05 pm |
| 6 3rd ♈ | 7 3rd ♈ ☽ v/c 12:13 am ☽ → ♉ 2:25 am | 3rd ♉ 4th Quarter 6:28 am ◑ | 9 4th ♉ ☽ v/c 6:39 am ☽ → ♊ 9:05 am |
| 13 4th ♋ | 14 4th ♋ ☽ v/c 3:46 am ☽ → ♌ 6:36 am | 15 4th ♌ | 4th ♌ ☽ v/c 5:38 am New Moon 5:38 am ☽ → ♍ 7:14 pm ● *New Moon* |
| 20 1st ♎ | 21 1st ♎ ☽ v/c 4:31 pm ☽ → ♏ 7:22 pm | 22 1st ♏ | 23 1st ♏ ☉ → ♍ 5:01 am ☿ ℞ 3:59 pm *Sun enters Virgo* *Mercury retrograde* |
| 27 2nd ♑ ♂ → ♎ 9:20 am | 28 2nd ♑ ☽ v/c 7:49 am ☽ → ≈ 10:32 am ♅ ℞ 10:39 pm | 29 2nd ≈ ☽ v/c 11:04 pm | 2nd ≈ ☽ → ♓ 9:56 am Full Moon 9:36 pm ○ *Blue Moon* |
| 3 | 4 | 5 | 6 |

Eastern Daylight Time (EDT)

**Zodiac Signs**

♈ Aries
♉ Taurus
♊ Gemini
♋ Cancer
♌ Leo
♍ Virgo
♎ Libra
♏ Scorpio
♐ Sagittarius
♑ Capricorn
≈ Aquarius
♓ Pisces

**Planets**

☉ Sun
☽ Moon
☿ Mercury
♀ Venus
♂ Mars
♃ Jupiter
♄ Saturn
♅ Uranus
♆ Neptune
♇ Pluto

# AUGUST 2023

| TH | F | SA | NOTES |
|---|---|---|---|
| 3rd ♓ 3 | 3rd ♓ 4<br>☽ v/c 9:21 pm<br>☽ → ♈ 11:19 pm | 3rd ♈ 5 | |
| 4th ♊ 10 | 4th ♊ 11<br>☽ v/c 1:27 pm<br>☽ → ♋ 6:52 pm | 4th ♋ 12 | |
| 1st ♍ 17 | 1st ♍ 18 | 1st ♍ 19<br>☽ v/c 4:51 am<br>☽ → ♎ 7:53 am | |
| 1st ♏ ◐<br>☽ v/c 1:10 am<br>☽ → ♐ 4:07 am<br>2nd Quarter 5:57 am | 2nd ♐ 25 | 2nd ♐ 26<br>☽ v/c 7:56 am<br>☽ → ♑ 9:05 am | |
| 3rd ♓ 31 | 1 | 2 | |
| 7 | 8 | 9 | |

### Aspects & Moon Phases

| | | | |
|---|---|---|---|
| ☌ Conjunction | 0° | ● New Moon | (1st Quarter) |
| ⚹ Sextile | 60° | ◐ Waxing Moon | (2nd Quarter) |
| □ Square | 90° | ○ Full Moon | (3rd Quarter) |
| △ Trine | 120° | ◑ Waning Moon | (4th Quarter) |
| ⊼ Quincunx | 150° | | |
| ☍ Opposition | 180° | | |

# SEPTEMBER 2023

| SU | M | T | W |
|---|---|---|---|
| 27 | 28 | 29 | 30 |
| 3 3rd ♈ ☽ v/c 7:57 am ☽ → ♉ 11:00 am ♀ D 9:20 pm | 4 3rd ♉ ♃ ℞ 10:10 am *Labor Day* | 5 3rd ♉ ☽ v/c 12:46 pm ☽ → ♊ 4:07 pm | 6 3rd ♊ 4th Quarter 6:21 pm ◑ |
| 10 4th ♋ ☽ v/c 8:47 am ☽ → ♌ 12:36 pm | 11 4th ♌ | 12 4th ♌ ☽ v/c 11:06 am | 13 4th ♌ ☽ → ♍ 1:18 am |
| 17 1st ♎ ☽ v/c 9:06 pm | 18 1st ♎ ☽ → ♏ 12:58 am | 19 1st ♏ | 20 1st ♏ ☽ v/c 6:21 am ☽ → ♐ 10:06 am |
| 24 2nd ♑ ☽ v/c 4:05 pm ☽ → ♒ 7:29 pm | 25 2nd ♒ | 26 2nd ♒ ☽ v/c 8:38 am ☽ → ♓ 8:18 pm | 27 2nd ♓ |
| 1 | 2 | 3 | 4 |

Eastern Daylight Time (EDT)

**Zodiac Signs**

♈ Aries ♌ Leo ♐ Sagittarius
♉ Taurus ♍ Virgo ♑ Capricorn
♊ Gemini ♎ Libra ♒ Aquarius
♋ Cancer ♏ Scorpio ♓ Pisces

**Planets**

☉ Sun ♃ Jupiter
☽ Moon ♄ Saturn
☿ Mercury ♅ Uranus
♀ Venus ♆ Neptune
♂ Mars ♇ Pluto

# SEPTEMBER 2023

| TH | F | SA | NOTES |
|---|---|---|---|
| 31 | 1<br>3rd ♓<br>☽ v/c 6:36 am<br>☽ → ♈ 9:25 am | 2<br>3rd ♈ | |
| 7<br>4th ♊<br>☽ v/c 6:22 pm | 8<br>4th ♊<br>☽ → ♋ 1:00 am | 9<br>4th ♋ | |
| ●<br>4th ♍<br>New Moon 9:40 pm<br>*New Moon* | 15<br>1st ♍<br>☽ v/c 9:49 am<br>☽ → ♎ 1:44 pm<br>☿ D 4:21 pm<br>*Mercury direct* | 16<br>1st ♎ | |
| 21<br>1st ♐ | ◐<br>1st ♐<br>☽ v/c 3:32 pm<br>2nd Quarter 3:32 pm<br>☽ → ♑ 4:20 pm | 23<br>2nd ♑<br>☉ → ♎ 2:50 am<br>*Mabon*<br>*Sun enters Libra*<br>*Fall Equinox* | |
| 28<br>2nd ♓<br>☽ v/c 4:58 pm<br>☽ → ♈ 8:17 pm | ○<br>2nd ♈<br>Full Moon 5:58 am<br>*Harvest Moon* | 30<br>3rd ♈<br>☽ v/c 5:50 pm<br>☽ → ♉ 9:18 pm | |
| 5 | 6 | 7 | |

**Aspects & Moon Phases**

- ☌ Conjunction 0°
- ⚹ Sextile 60°
- □ Square 90°
- △ Trine 120°
- ⚻ Quincunx 150°
- ☍ Opposition 180°

- ● New Moon (1st Quarter)
- ◐ Waxing Moon (2nd Quarter)
- ○ Full Moon (3rd Quarter)
- ◑ Waning Moon (4th Quarter)

# OCTOBER 2023

| SU | M | T | W |
|---|---|---|---|
| 1<br>3rd ♉ | 2<br>3rd ♉<br>☽ v/c 9:20 pm | 3<br>3rd ♉<br>☽ → ♊ 1:03 am | 4<br>3rd ♊<br>☿ → ♎ 8:09 pm |
| 8<br>4th ♌<br>♀ → ♍ 9:11 pm | 9<br>4th ♌ | 10<br>4th ♌<br>☽ v/c 5:37 am<br>☽ → ♍ 8:02 am<br>♇ D 9:10 pm | 11<br>4th ♍ |
| 15<br>1st ♎<br>☽ v/c 3:01 am<br>☽ → ♏ 7:04 am | 16<br>1st ♏ | 17<br>1st ♏<br>☽ v/c 11:44 am<br>☽ → ♐ 3:36 pm | 18<br>1st ♐ |
| 22<br>2nd ♑<br>☽ v/c 2:00 am<br>☽ → ♒ 2:06 am<br>☿ → ♏ 2:49 am | 23<br>2nd ♒<br>☉ → ♏ 12:21 pm<br>☽ v/c 3:04 pm<br>*Sun enters Scorpio* | 24<br>2nd ♒<br>☽ → ♓ 4:33 am | 25<br>2nd ♓ |
| 29<br>3rd ♉ | 30<br>3rd ♉<br>☽ v/c 7:36 am<br>☽ → ♊ 11:08 am | 31<br>3rd ♊<br>*Samhain*<br>*Halloween* | 1 |
| 5 | 6 | 7 | 8 |

Eastern Daylight Time (EDT)

**Zodiac Signs**

♈ Aries
♉ Taurus
♊ Gemini
♋ Cancer
♌ Leo
♍ Virgo
♎ Libra
♏ Scorpio
♐ Sagittarius
♑ Capricorn
♒ Aquarius
♓ Pisces

**Planets**

☉ Sun
☽ Moon
☿ Mercury
♀ Venus
♂ Mars
♃ Jupiter
♄ Saturn
♅ Uranus
♆ Neptune
♇ Pluto

# OCTOBER 2023

| TH | F | SA | NOTES |
|---|---|---|---|
| 5<br>3rd ♊<br>☽ v/c 2:34 am<br>☽ → ♋ 8:32 am | 6<br>3rd ♋<br>4th Quarter 9:48 am ◑ | 7<br>4th ♋<br>☽ v/c 3:12 pm<br>☽ → ♌ 7:24 pm | |
| 12<br>4th ♍<br>♂ → ♏ 12:04 am<br>☽ v/c 4:10 pm<br>☽ → ♎ 8:22 pm | 13<br>4th ♎ | 14<br>4th ♎<br>New Moon 1:55 pm ●<br>*Solar Eclipse/ New Moon* | |
| 19<br>1st ♐<br>☽ v/c 3:02 pm<br>☽ → ♑ 9:55 pm | 20<br>1st ♑ | 21<br>1st ♑<br>2nd Quarter 11:29 pm ◐ | |
| 26<br>2nd ♓<br>☽ v/c 2:39 am<br>☽ → ♈ 6:02 am | 27<br>2nd ♈ | 28<br>2nd ♈<br>☽ v/c 4:20 am<br>☽ → ♉ 7:44 am<br>Full Moon 4:24 pm ○<br>*Lunar Eclipse/ Blood Moon* | |
| 2 | 3 | 4 | |
| 9 | 10 | 11 | |

### Aspects & Moon Phases

|  |  |  |  |
|---|---|---|---|
| ☌ Conjunction | 0° | ● New Moon | (1st Quarter) |
| ⚹ Sextile | 60° | ◐ Waxing Moon | (2nd Quarter) |
| □ Square | 90° | ○ Full Moon | (3rd Quarter) |
| △ Trine | 120° | ◑ Waning Moon | (4th Quarter) |
| ⚻ Quincunx | 150° | | |
| ☍ Opposition | 180° | | |

# NOVEMBER 2023

| SU | M | T | W |
|---|---|---|---|
| 29 | 30 | 31 | 1<br>3rd ♊<br>☽ v/c 8:36 am<br>☽ → ♋ 5:30 pm |
| 5<br>3rd ♌<br>EST in effect 2:00 am<br>4th Quarter 3:37 am<br>*Daylight Saving Time ends at 2:00 am* | 6<br>4th ♌<br>☽ v/c 2:25 am<br>☽ → ♍ 2:39 pm | 7<br>4th ♍<br>*Election Day (general)* | 8<br>4th ♍<br>♀ → ♎ 4:30 am<br>☽ v/c 11:55 pm |
| 12<br>4th ♏ | 13<br>4th ♏<br>New Moon 4:27 am<br>☽ v/c 6:03 pm<br>☽ → ♐ 9:23 pm<br>*New Moon* | 14<br>1st ♐ | 15<br>1st ♐<br>☽ v/c 5:57 pm |
| 19<br>1st ♒ | 20<br>1st ♒<br>☽ v/c 5:50 am<br>2nd Quarter 5:50 am<br>☽ → ♓ 9:29 am | 21<br>2nd ♓ | 22<br>2nd ♓<br>☉ → ♐ 9:03 am<br>☽ v/c 10:10 am<br>☽ → ♈ 12:19 pm<br>*Sun enters Sagittarius* |
| 26<br>2nd ♉<br>☽ v/c 4:52 pm<br>☽ → ♊ 7:40 pm | 27<br>2nd ♊<br>Full Moon 4:16 am<br>*Mourning Moon* | 28<br>3rd ♊<br>☽ v/c 8:03 pm | 29<br>3rd ♊<br>☽ → ♋ 1:54 am |
| 3 | 4 | 5 | 6 |

Eastern Daylight Time (EDT) becomes Eastern Standard Time (EST) November 5

ZODIAC SIGNS

♈ Aries
♉ Taurus
♊ Gemini
♋ Cancer
♌ Leo
♍ Virgo
♎ Libra
♏ Scorpio
♐ Sagittarius
♑ Capricorn
♒ Aquarius
♓ Pisces

PLANETS

☉ Sun
☽ Moon
☿ Mercury
♀ Venus
♂ Mars
♃ Jupiter
♄ Saturn
♅ Uranus
♆ Neptune
♇ Pluto

# NOVEMBER 2023

| TH | F | SA | NOTES |
|---|---|---|---|
| 3rd ♋ 2 | 3rd ♋ 3<br>☽ v/c 11:28 pm | 3rd ♋ 4<br>♄ D 3:03 am<br>☽ → ♌ 3:21 am | |
| 4th ♍ 9<br>☽ → ♎ 3:08 am | 4th ♎ 10<br>☿ → ♐ 1:25 am | 4th ♎ 11<br>☽ v/c 10:05 am<br>☽ → ♏ 1:39 pm<br>*Veterans Day* | |
| 1st ♐ 16<br>☽ → ♑ 2:41 am | 1st ♑ 17 | 1st ♑ 18<br>☽ v/c 3:27 am<br>☽ → ♒ 6:28 am | |
| 2nd ♈ 23<br>*Thanksgiving Day* | 2nd ♈ 24<br>♂ → ♐ 5:15 am<br>☽ v/c 12:40 pm<br>☽ → ♉ 3:29 pm | 2nd ♉ 25 | |
| 3rd ♋ 30 | 1 | 2 | |
| 7 | 8 | 9 | |

### Aspects & Moon Phases

| | | | |
|---|---|---|---|
| ☌ Conjunction | 0° | ● New Moon | (1st Quarter) |
| ⚹ Sextile | 60° | ◐ Waxing Moon | (2nd Quarter) |
| □ Square | 90° | ○ Full Moon | (3rd Quarter) |
| △ Trine | 120° | ◑ Waning Moon | (4th Quarter) |
| ⚻ Quincunx | 150° | | |
| ☍ Opposition | 180° | | |

# DECEMBER 2023

| SU | M | T | W |
|---|---|---|---|
| 26 | 27 | 28 | 29 |
| 3<br>3rd ♌<br>☽ v/c 9:11 pm<br>☽ → ♍ 10:50 pm | 4<br>3rd ♍<br>♀ → ♏ 1:51 pm | 3rd ♍<br>4th Quarter 12:49 am | 6<br>4th ♍<br>♆ D 8:20 am<br>☽ v/c 8:50 am<br>☽ → ♎ 11:35 am |
| 10<br>4th ♏ | 11<br>4th ♏<br>☽ v/c 3:57 am<br>☽ → ♐ 6:11 am | 4th ♐<br>New Moon 6:32 pm<br>*New Moon* | 13<br>1st ♐<br>☽ v/c 1:48 am<br>☿ ℞ 2:09 am<br>☽ → ♑ 10:31 am<br>*Mercury retrograde* |
| 17<br>1st ♒<br>☽ v/c 7:04 am<br>☽ → ♓ 2:58 pm | 18<br>1st ♓ | 1st ♓<br>2nd Quarter 1:39 pm<br>☽ v/c 4:03 pm<br>☽ → ♈ 5:47 pm | 20<br>2nd ♈ |
| 24<br>2nd ♉<br>☽ v/c 1:40 am<br>☽ → ♊ 3:15 am<br>*Christmas Eve* | 25<br>2nd ♊<br>*Christmas Day* | 2nd ♊<br>☽ v/c 2:55 am<br>☽ → ♋ 10:15 am<br>Full Moon 7:33 pm<br>*Kwanzaa begins*<br>*Long Nights Moon* | 27<br>3rd ♋ |
| 31<br>3rd ♌<br>☽ v/c 12:18 am<br>☽ → ♍ 6:53 am<br>*New Year's Eve* | 1 | 2 | 3 |

Eastern Standard Time (EST)

**Zodiac Signs**

♈ Aries
♉ Taurus
♊ Gemini
♋ Cancer
♌ Leo
♍ Virgo
♎ Libra
♏ Scorpio
♐ Sagittarius
♑ Capricorn
♒ Aquarius
♓ Pisces

**Planets**

☉ Sun
☽ Moon
☿ Mercury
♀ Venus
♂ Mars
♃ Jupiter
♄ Saturn
♅ Uranus
♆ Neptune
♇ Pluto

# DECEMBER 2023

| TH | F | SA | NOTES |
|---|---|---|---|
| 30 | 1<br>3rd ♋<br>☽ v/c 8:07 am<br>☿ → ♑ 9:31 am<br>☽ → ♌ 11:00 am | 2<br>3rd ♌ | |
| 7<br>4th ♎ | 8<br>4th ♎<br>☽ v/c 8:05 pm<br>☽ → ♏ 10:35 pm | 9<br>4th ♏ | |
| 14<br>1st ♑ | 15<br>1st ♑<br>☽ v/c 11:04 am<br>☽ → ♒ 12:56 pm | 16<br>1st ♒ | |
| 21<br>2nd ♈<br>☽ v/c 9:47 pm<br>☽ → ♉ 9:50 pm<br>☉ → ♑ 10:27 pm<br>*Yule*<br>*Sun enters Capricorn*<br>*Winter Solstice* | 22<br>2nd ♉ | 23<br>2nd ♉<br>☿ → ♐ 1:18 am | |
| 28<br>3rd ♋<br>☽ v/c 5:57 pm<br>☽ → ♌ 7:23 pm | 29<br>3rd ♌<br>♀ → ♐ 3:24 pm | 30<br>3rd ♌<br>♃ D 9:40 pm | |
| 4 | 5 | 6 | |

### Aspects & Moon Phases

| | | | |
|---|---|---|---|
| ☌ Conjunction | 0° | ● New Moon | (1st Quarter) |
| ⚹ Sextile | 60° | ◐ Waxing Moon | (2nd Quarter) |
| □ Square | 90° | ○ Full Moon | (3rd Quarter) |
| △ Trine | 120° | ◑ Waning Moon | (4th Quarter) |
| ⚻ Quincunx | 150° | | |
| ☍ Opposition | 180° | | |